# NILE

# NILE

MARTHA HOLMES

GAVIN MAXWELL

TIM SCOONES

BBC
BOOKS

This book is published to accompany the television series *Nile*, first broadcast on BBC2 in 2004
Series producer: Martha Holmes
Executive producer: Mike Gunton

Published by BBC Books, BBC Worldwide Ltd, Woodlands, 80 Wood Lane, London W12 0TT

First published 2004

ISBN 0 563 48713 5

Commissioning editors: Shirley Patton and Nicky Ross
Project editor: Martin Redfern
Art director: Linda Blakemore
Designer: Bobby Birchall (DW Design)

Picture researcher: Deirdre O'Day
Production controller: Christopher Tinker

Set in Helvetica Neue and Trajan
Printed and bound in Great Britain by Butler & Tanner Ltd, Frome
Colour separations by Radstock Reproductions Ltd, Midsomer Norton
Jacket printed by Lawrence-Allen Ltd, Weston-super-Mare

*FROM MARTHA*
*To Frank, whose support and love have been as*
*steady as the Nile itself*


*FROM GAVIN*
*To Mags, Zia and my parents for inspiring, supporting and*
*enduring my curiosity*


*FROM TIM*
*To the gentle, kind and gracious people of the Nile, who*
*welcomed me into their amazing world*

Left: Lake Tana is a huge reservoir for the Blue Nile's waters in the centre of Ethiopia's Highlands. It was formed 30 million years ago when a flow of molten volcanic rock dammed the end of a high mountain basin.

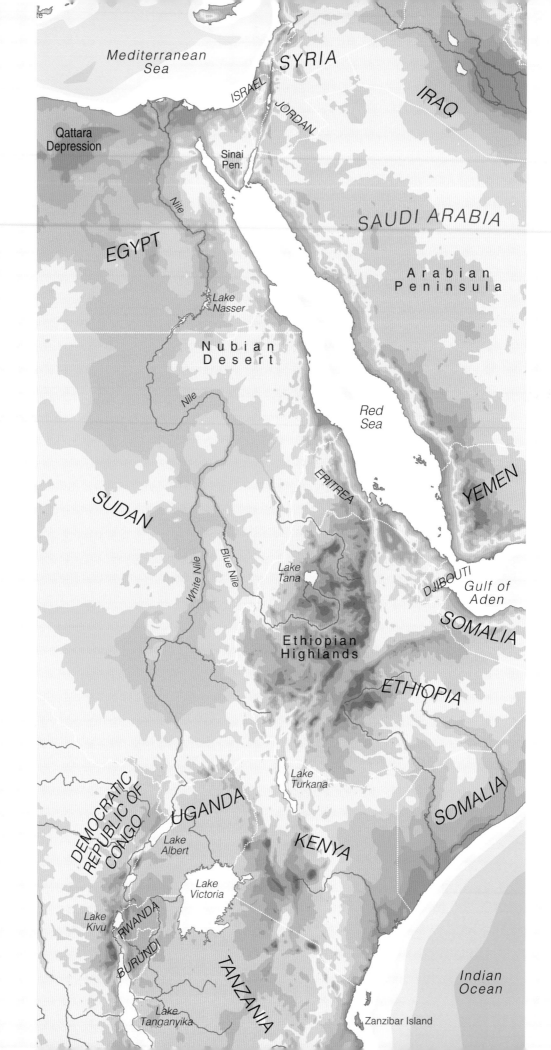

Mediterranean
Sea

SYRIA

IRAQ

ISRAEL

JORDAN

Qattara
Depression

Sinai
Pen.

SAUDI ARABIA

Nile

EGYPT

Arabian
Peninsula

Lake
Nasser

Nubian
Desert

Nile

Red
Sea

YEMEN

ERITREA

SUDAN

White Nile

Blue Nile

Lake
Tana

DJIBOUTI

Gulf of
Aden

SOMALIA

Ethiopian
Highlands

ETHIOPIA

Lake
Turkana

DEMOCRATIC
REPUBLIC OF
CONGO

UGANDA

SOMALIA

Lake
Albert

KENYA

Lake
Victoria

Lake
Kivu

RWANDA

BURUNDI

TANZANIA

Indian
Ocean

10

Lake
Tanganyika

Zanzibar Island

# INTRODUCTION

The Nile is the longest river in the world. Stretching for approximately 6700 km (4160 miles), it drains more than 3 million sq. km (1.15 million square miles), or 10 per cent, of Africa and some of its water takes six months to reach the sea. Remarkably, although it flows through one of the harshest deserts on earth and travels the last 2400 km (1500 miles) without a single tributary to assist its steady passage north, it never runs dry.

The river has two main arms that stretch into Africa: the White Nile and the Blue Nile. The longer of these is the White Nile, which starts its journey in the heart of the continent among a collection of lakes and mountains. Lake Victoria, the largest lake in Africa, feeds the Victoria Nile which flows through Kyoga, a secondary swampy lake, to Lake Albert. Here its waters are joined by those of the Semliki, which springs from Lakes George and Edward. The river that flows north from Lake Albert is the White Nile. This entire lake region is interlaced with streams and rivers, all of which drain to one or other of the lakes. Rising high in the middle of the area is the Ruwenzori range of mountains, known throughout history as the 'Mountains of the Moon'. Surrounded in almost permanent cloud, they remained unseen by European eyes for decades after the first explorers had discovered the main lakes.

As the White Nile pours out of Lake Albert it leaves the wet, tropical forests of central Africa and heads into a more arid zone. It passes through a rocky, mountainous region that renders the river virtually unnavigable, and then enters an immense, near-impenetrable swamp – the Sudd. About half the water that pours out of the lake region of central Africa evaporates as it travels slowly through this area. Once out of the swamp, the White Nile is joined by a tributary – the Sobat – whose waters originate in Ethiopia. Finally, at the city of Khartoum the Blue Nile joins forces with the White Nile and the river simply becomes the Nile. After steering an S-shaped course through the Nubian massif and down six cataracts, or rapids, it heads directly north, entering the Mediterranean Sea as a spreading delta at Alexandria.

The geography of the Nile is extraordinary, but it is not this that has made its name so familiar to us; it is its association with the world of ancient Egypt. Emerging some 3000 years before the birth of Christ, this civilization was fostered by the Nile and was entirely dependent on it. Ancient Egypt was creative and complex, and its achievements in art and architecture still have the power to astonish visitors. But although its people depended utterly on the Nile for their survival, they did surprisingly little to find out about its character upstream. Instead, they simply accepted that they were blessed by the river and, by extension, by the gods who had created their world for them.

Living on the banks of the Nile, the Egyptians were content with a developing society that was safe and offered luxuries unknown in the world outside their valley. But they recognized that they relied on two important features of the river. First, it flowed year-round and provided them with more than enough water to irrigate their crops and maintain themselves and their animals. Second, an immense flood came once a year, depositing a layer of highly fertile black soil on the flood plain. As the flood subsided and the river retreated, farmers followed in its wake, planting their crops in the life-giving mud. The Egyptians did not have to clear their land or plough and, according to the Greek historian Herodotus, they had it easy. In the fifth century BC he wrote: 'It is certain, however, that now they gather in fruit from the earth with less labour than any other men.'

It is this spectacular flood that sets the Nile apart from the other great rivers of the world. For just a few weeks every year it swells to 400 times its dry-season size, and carries with it a staggering 140 million tonnes of rich, fertile silt as it rages, thick and brown, towards the sea. For 5000 years Egyptians, both ancient and modern, relied on these gifts of water and soil to bring life to an otherwise barren desert world. And the Nile delivered them with great reliability. Only in the last century did this change. As a growing modern society, Egypt demanded more and more from the Nile, and waiting for the inundation seemed outdated. In 1902 the British built a dam at Aswan, but the flood was only fully brought under control in Egypt with the completion, upstream, of the Aswan High Dam in 1970. This impressive feat of engineering guarantees year-round irrigation of crops and more electricity than the country can use, but it comes at a cost. The rich silt from Ethiopia now builds up in Lake Nasser, behind the dam, and as a result Egypt has to import fertilizers for the fields of the Nile valley.

The flood originates in the Blue Nile, in one of the most beautiful mountainous regions on earth: the Ethiopian Highlands. In summer, heavy rains drench the slopes of the mountains and a powerful force of water builds up. Loosened by the activities of rodents and farmers, the black, volcanic soil is eroded and carried away by the river's headwaters. This is what brought fertility

**Above:** The Nile's rich silt and regular floods had the power to turn one of the world's harshest deserts into agricultural land so fertile that its abundant crops could support a great civilization.

to the arid, desert climate of ancient Egypt. By the time their civilization came to an end in the fourth century BC the ancient Egyptians knew about the Ethiopian Highlands, but they still preferred to attribute the flood to supernatural causes. And, prevented from exploring the Nile much beyond Aswan by the river's cataracts, they also preferred to believe that it was divine providence that gave it its steady year-round flow.

Cataracts, the Sudd, an inhospitable climate and hostile tribes continued to frustrate exploration of the Nile for some 2000 years after the collapse of the ancient Egyptian civilization. Indeed, as late as the eighteenth century, Europeans based their knowledge of the White Nile's source on a map by the Greek geographer Ptolemy that dated back to the second century AD. It was only in the nineteenth century that the map began to be redrawn.

The search for the source of the White Nile, led mostly by British gentlemen, was one of the most extraordinary chapters in human exploration. Journeys lasted for years, not months, and the explorers endured hardships that are unimaginable today. On returning from their travels into the heart of Africa they became household names in Victorian Britain: Burton, Speke, Baker, Livingstone and Stanley. Although personal rivalries were fierce, their expeditions built up knowledge of the geography of the White Nile's sources in modern-day Burundi, Rwanda, Uganda, Tanzania and Kenya. By the end of the nineteenth century the question of where the river comes from was 'settled' in geographical terms.

Today archaeologists, anthropologists and geographers continue to make discoveries about the river and its valley. But, running its course through the homelands of so many peoples, through so many strikingly different habitats – and through so much human history – the Nile will always retain some of its mystery.

**Right:** People living on the banks of the Nile have made boats out of papyrus for centuries. Timeless scenes like this can still be witnessed all along the length of the river.

**Overleaf:** The huge Blue Nile gorge cuts a steep gash through the high plateau of the Ethiopian Highlands. A few weeks of heavy rain give rise to a host of short-lived yet spectacular waterfalls.

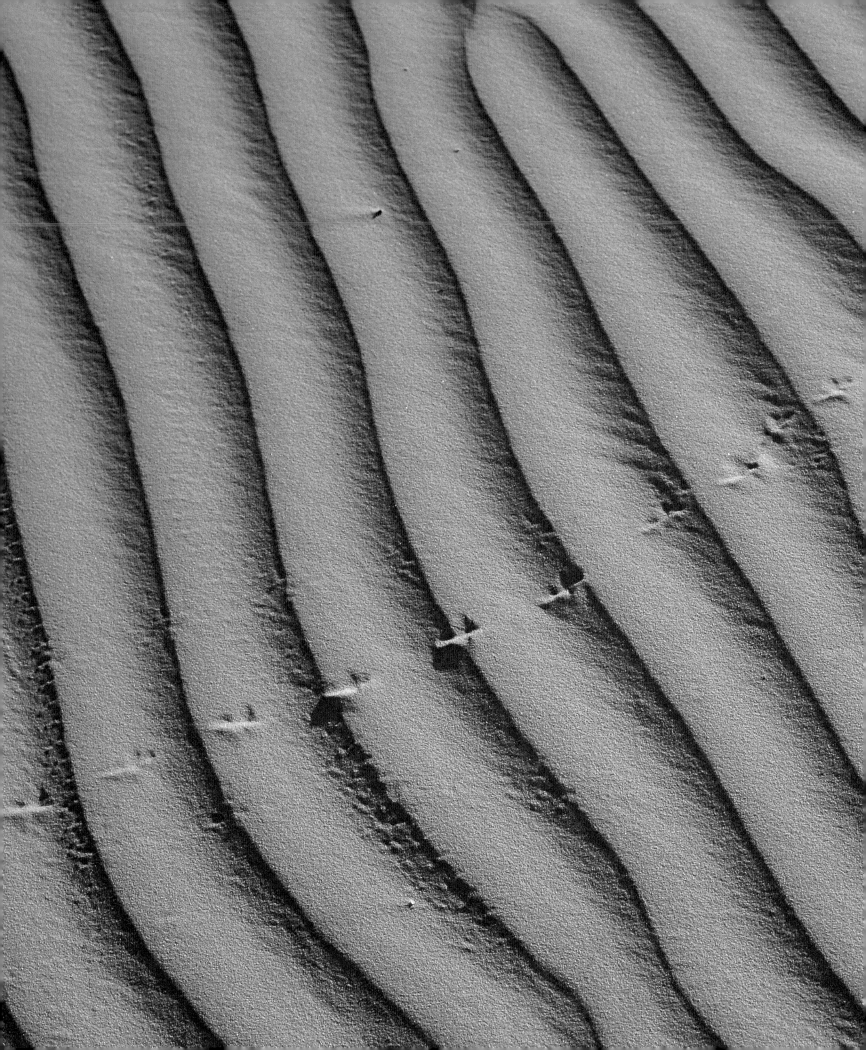

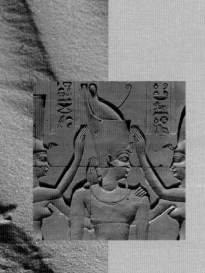

CHAPTER 1

# ANCIENT EGYPT

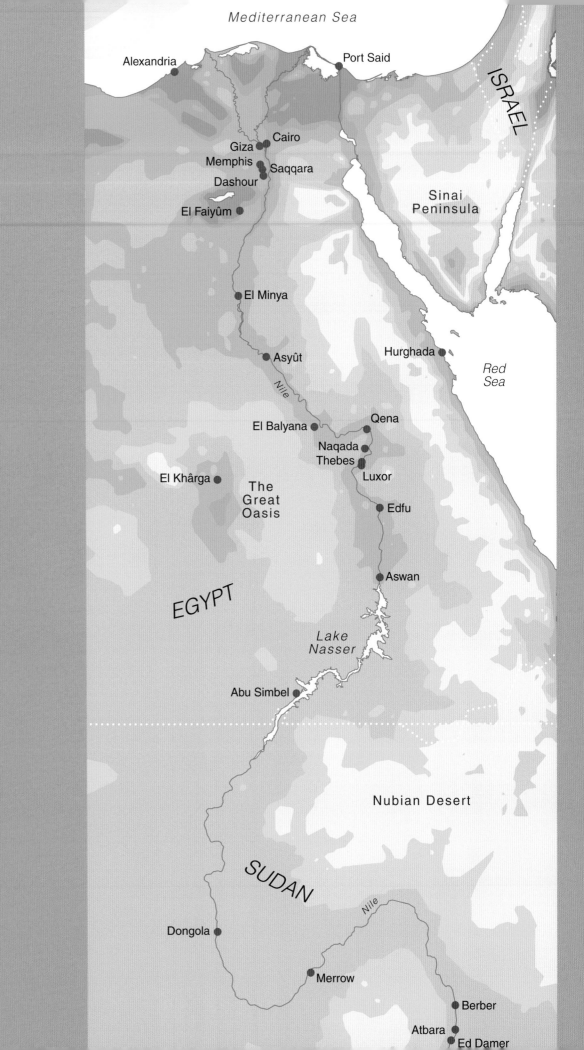

Above: The 'weighing of
the heart' in the presence
of Osiris. The heart of the
deceased must remain in
balance with justice and
order – or risk annihilation.

In the total darkness of an ancient tomb a vivid painting, exquisite in its execution yet
nightmarish in its content, lay hidden for thousands of years. It shows a figure with a green
face, its body tightly wrapped in white linen, watching impassively as a dog-headed beast
holds out a set of scales. The scales contain a feather on one side, and on the other a human
heart. A crocodile-headed monster crouches expectantly at the foot of the scales, ready to eat
the heart. Meanwhile, a bird-headed creature systematically writes down the result of this
demonic experiment. What could this dreadful tableau possibly mean? This is just one of many
tantalizing scenes from the art of ancient Egypt, a civilization so extraordinary that people have
seriously considered that it may have had a connection to another world.

A journey up the Nile leads the traveller back through time to the very heart of this supernatural
universe. Away from the neon and high-rises of Cairo there is a landscape strewn with
astonishing monuments created in the age of the pharaohs. This age – the dynastic period –

began 5000 years ago and lasted nearly 3000 years through three distinct periods: the Old, Middle and New Kingdoms. No subsequent civilization has endured as long, and no ancient civilization has left so many monuments.

Modern Cairo's greedy urban sprawl is brought up short by the pyramids of Giza, which dominate the neighbouring land. These monuments – one of the seven wonders of the ancient world – encapsulate much of ancient Egypt's character. Built with over 2 million limestone blocks, the Great Pyramid is still the world's heaviest building, weighing some 6 million tonnes. At 147 m (482 feet) high, it was also the tallest until the Eiffel Tower was erected in Paris in the nineteenth century. Yet, despite its magnificent dimensions, this 4500-year-old construction is built to an accuracy of just a few centimetres. The pyramids of Giza – and their predecessors at Saqqara and Dashour – reveal more than just a people's astonishing architectural prowess and precision: they also demonstrate a civilization's ability to mobilize labour on an unprecedented scale.

Continue south along the Nile and the land is divided into a lattice of fields that must look much as they did in dynastic times. The patchwork is punctuated with ancient monuments, the greatest of which is the vast temple complex of Karnak at Luxor, a forest of stone large enough

**Above:** The Nile carves its way through the bright lights of Cairo – a world away from the ordered landscape of ancient Egypt.

**Opposite:** Saqqara, the 'step' pyramid. Built for the pharaoh Djoser in c.2650 BC, this became the blueprint for all subsequent pyramids.

**Overleaf:** The pyramids at Giza still dominate the landscape and appear to have halted Cairo's growth.

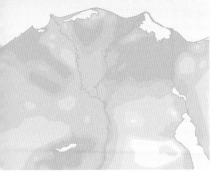

to contain ten cathedrals. On the western bank of the river, the seated colossi of Memnon keep watch in front of desolate mountains that are home to thousands of tombs hewn from rock. This is the Valley of the Kings, where Tutankhamun lay hidden for nearly 3500 years. Further south along the river one passes through Aswan, where the sand dunes of the desert appear frozen in time, on the point of subsiding and smothering the water. At the southern end of Egypt, on the border with modern-day Sudan, is the temple of Abu Simbel. Here the imposing

**Above:** The colossi of Memnon on the western bank of the Nile originally stood at the entrance to a massive mortuary temple complex. The rising Nile floodwaters frequently used to lap their toes.

figures, carved into the rock and over 3000 years old, remain defiant in the face of the changing

world around them. All these wonders and marvels lie within sight of the Nile. The river itself is

the heart of Egypt, a silent witness to thousands of years of human experience. As Herodotus,

an inexhaustible traveller and chronicler of the ancient world, wrote in the fifth century BC:

'Egypt is the Gift of the Nile.'

**Above:** Medinet Habu, Luxor – a typical temple of the New Kingdom. The sandstone walls are decorated with images of the pharaoh smiting his opponents.

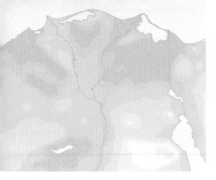

It is relatively recently that we have begun to understand the beliefs and culture of ancient Egypt. Its hieroglyphics – a vivid pictorial script and one of the earliest forms of writing – started to be deciphered only in 1822, following the discovery of the Rosetta Stone, whose parallel inscriptions in Greek and hieroglyphics gave scholars the key to the meaning of the hieroglyphic language. Once this bizarre form of writing had been deciphered, the strange stories it told raised interest around the world. And such is our fascination with ancient Egypt that even today each new discovery about its civilization, each scrap of new information, makes headline news.

**Below:** The town of Aswan once marked the southern boundary of ancient Egypt thanks to a series of rocky cataracts upstream, which formed a natural barrier.

# THE BIRTH OF CIVILIZATION

Once people began settling along the Nile, Egypt flourished into an increasingly sophisticated civilization. But, contrary to popular belief, ancient Egypt was not the world's first civilization. This occurred in Mesopotamia (now Iraq), a region defined by not one but two rivers: the Euphrates and the Tigris. The land between these rivers was the southern part of an area known as the Fertile Crescent, once a vast, lush region that also encompassed Palestine, southern Turkey and Iran. In about 9000 BC the single most important social change in human history began to sweep through this crescent: the Neolithic revolution. During this period people began to abandon their hunter-gatherer lifestyles to take up agriculture, which allowed them some control over their environment. The reward was considerable: a potential surplus of food. This change was to have a profound effect on the social fabric of the human race. Until then, each hunter-gatherer had needed about 400 hectares (1000 acres) to support a family. Farmers now needed just 10 hectares (25 acres). The result of a virtually assured food supply, and a probable surplus, led to the formation of densely populated, permanent settlements.

**Above:** Abu Simbel. The construction of the Aswan dam risked submerging this massive temple complex, so, in 1964, it had to be dismantled and relocated 60 m (200 feet) up the valley side.

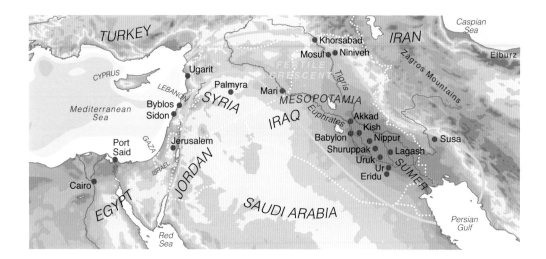

In terms of human history, the Neolithic revolution was a speedy affair in the Fertile Crescent. In the course of just 1000 years, tiny temporary villages became 4-hectare (10-acre) settlements contained within fortified walls. Irrigation systems enabled people to exploit and manage the flow of water over their fields in order to maximize crop yields. By about 3500 BC the early farming settlements between the fertile banks of the Euphrates and Tigris had flourished to become a series of independent city-states. Here skills and ideas developed; social structures and systems of government and religious belief grew in complexity; and writing was invented. This was the Sumerian civilization – the world's first.

While the Fertile Crescent was undergoing a revolution, archaeological records show that Egypt was moving at a different pace. Despite its inherent suitability for agriculture, the Nile valley appears to have resisted early Neolithic intrusions, and farming started thousands of years after the first cultivated fields appeared in Mesopotamia. The peoples of Egypt were content to remain hunter-gatherers. This was probably because the North African landscape of 9000 BC was dramatically different from the parched expanse we know today. At that time it enjoyed annual monsoon rains. The result was a landscape that was a combination of forest and lush green savannah, home to abundant animals. The heavy rainfall meant that the vastly swollen Nile was a giant, shifting marsh. Although the river provided fresh water and fish, people did not need to settle close to it while there was so much game in the surrounding land. Even if they had been aware of new forms of land use, they would have had little need for them.

However, in about 6400 BC the climate of Egypt started to become more arid. As the monsoon rains dried up, the savannah shrank and the sand spread. Within a few generations people

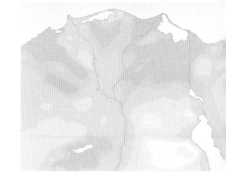

were forced to change their way of life. Fortuitously, the precarious marshy areas of the Nile began to dry out at the same time, creating a more benign environment for humans. The Nile valley started to be settled.

Climate change was not, of course, instantaneous and for a period Egypt was a semi-arid region. At this time its native peoples could survive by hunting during certain seasons of the year while also exploiting small pockets of vegetation. But the process of desertification was inexorable and the population clustering around the Nile was forced to find a new way of living and co-operating. By about 5000 BC nomads from North Africa had settled permanently along the river. Meanwhile, farmers were migrating from an overpopulated Mesopotamia to the Nile's northern delta. An intriguing hybrid was created: a hunting-gathering culture, based around a riverine habitat, coexisting with a farming tradition from the Fertile Crescent. It was the beginning of a new type of civilization.

Below: Thanks to the Nile a narrow, fertile strip stretches the length of Egypt. The grids of fields look similar to how they would have done in pharaonic times.

The Sumerians, their city-states in Mesopotamia lying precariously on a giant marsh, tried to reclaim their land from water. But it was at the mercy of two great rivers that were subject to frequent devastating floods and this sabotaged progress. Much of the archaeological record has simply been washed away. The Nile valley, on the other hand, was a stable flood plain fed by one river. Although agriculture started later there, it probably gave a richer return. The Nile people leapfrogged the city-state phase of social evolution and progressed quickly from local village communities to two large kingdoms: Upper Egypt and Lower Egypt. Then, in about 3000 BC, Upper Egypt subsumed Lower Egypt and dynastic Egypt was born. Now civilization was defined not by the walls of a city but by the geographical boundaries of a single united country with one king.

## A UNIVERSAL ORDER

From a satellite the path of the Nile is clearly visible – a ribbon of fertile land, defiant against the endless expanses of surrounding desert. Its shape resembles a lotus flower: the stem is the valley (Upper Egypt), 1060 km (660 miles) long and for much of it just a few kilometres wide. The flower is the delta (Lower Egypt), a vast marshy expanse where the river finally meets the Mediterranean.

**Opposite:** The Sahara was once a fertile savannah, full of life. An intense arid period transformed this landscape for ever, along with the fortunes of its people and wildlife.

**Below:** A satellite view of Egypt reveals the Nile's distinctive lotus shape. Upper Egypt is the southern valley stem; Lower Egypt is the northern delta flower.

Left: Papyrus was abundant throughout ancient Egypt. It was both a haven for wildlife and the raw material for scribes. Papyrus scrolls have been a vital source of information about life along the Nile.

Much of the greenery in the delta and along the banks of the river is made up of a reed that is inextricably associated with the ancient Egyptians: papyrus. In their hands, strips of papyrus were interwoven and compressed to make sheets. These were pasted together into long rolls, which could be written or painted on. It is the records on surviving papyrus scrolls that provide us with much of our knowledge about the land of the pharaohs.

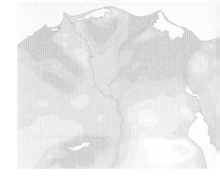

When drawing, whether on papyrus or on the walls of tombs or temples, ancient Egypt's artists portrayed their subjects as clearly as possible, in their most characteristic forms. This explains the somewhat eccentric-looking images in Egyptian art – a combination of profile, semi-profile and frontal views. Every aspect of life was drawn with such truthfulness that today zoologists can recognize the exact species of birds and animals that lived on the banks of the Nile. But this was no arbitrary process. The artists adhered to strict rules that endured for 3000 years – the longest-lived 'style' in the history of art.

**Above:** Relief from the Temple of Hatshepsut in Luxor. Fishing was a highly productive activity thanks to a never-ending supply of catfish, perch, tilapia and carp.

**Left:** This relief from the Temple of Horus in Edfu shows the pharaoh wearing the double crown of Upper and Lower Egypt, symbolizing the unification of both lands.

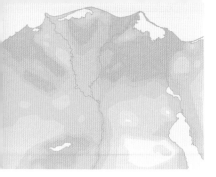

Ancient Egyptians saw the vivid colours of the sky mirrored in the Nile below, so they deduced that the heavens were composed of water. They thought water surrounded the earth and extended infinitely outwards in all directions. The world itself existed as a cosmic bubble floating within a vast ocean, and all life was contained within that bubble. Their land was aligned to the four points of the compass. They believed the Nile had its source in underground seas and erupted from the depths in the south, at Aswan. The river then travelled north towards the circumpolar stars (the Egyptians called them 'imperishable' because they never set below the horizon). Lying just 30 degrees above the horizon, these stars were thought to lie along the edge of a celestial ocean, much as papyrus reeds line the banks of the Nile.

It was thought that in the sky above, the sun traversed this watery realm in a kind of solar boat, navigating a course from east to west to cross the Nile. At the end of the day the sun set in the western desert, appearing to die as the sky turned red, purple, then black. At night it remained within the cosmic void, travelling in its boat through an underworld place – the Duat. This was divided into 12 'rooms', one for each hour of the night. Throughout the night the stars above appeared to mirror the Nile below: the Milky Way was seen as a series of islands in the midst of celestial waters, just as islands were seen on the river each year as the flood receded. As the black sky began to turn orange the following morning, the sun reappeared on the horizon of the eastern desert. It was, for the ancient Egyptians, a continual cycle of death and renewal.

The boundaries of their world were fairly clearly defined. In the north the Mediterranean obstructed travel – the ancient Egyptians were never great seafarers. To the east lay mountain ranges, the Sinai desert and the Red Sea. In the south the majestic Nile became a frothing torrent running through granite cliffs. And in the west the barren Sahara desert was a threat to life itself. Here temperatures on the summer sand can be a foot-roasting $58^{\circ}$C ($136^{\circ}$F). Egypt was effectively barricaded, so in the minds of its people it became a sealed and insulated land. Within its ordered boundaries they had all they needed. Outside existed a world of chaos. They, the Egyptians, were 'people'; the inhabitants of the rest of the world were inferior beings.

**Opposite:** Astral ceiling from the burial chamber of Seti I. Egyptians divided day and night equally into 12 hours, with the major constellations represented as mythological characters and creatures.

# THE REPLENISHING FLOOD

Safe within the natural boundaries of their land, the Egyptians knew they relied for their prosperity on one big annual event: the Nile's flood. In a land of meagre rainfall, this was vital and came to dominate the rhythm of the year. The Nile is one of the most reliable river systems in the world, and the Egyptians saw in the flood the same cycle of death and renewal that they saw in the daily passage of the sun. The river's movements were closely studied and recorded, and in their efforts to understand and predict the flood's arrival they produced a zodiac (the blueprint for the one consulted today) and a calendar that divided the year into 12 months grouped into three seasons.

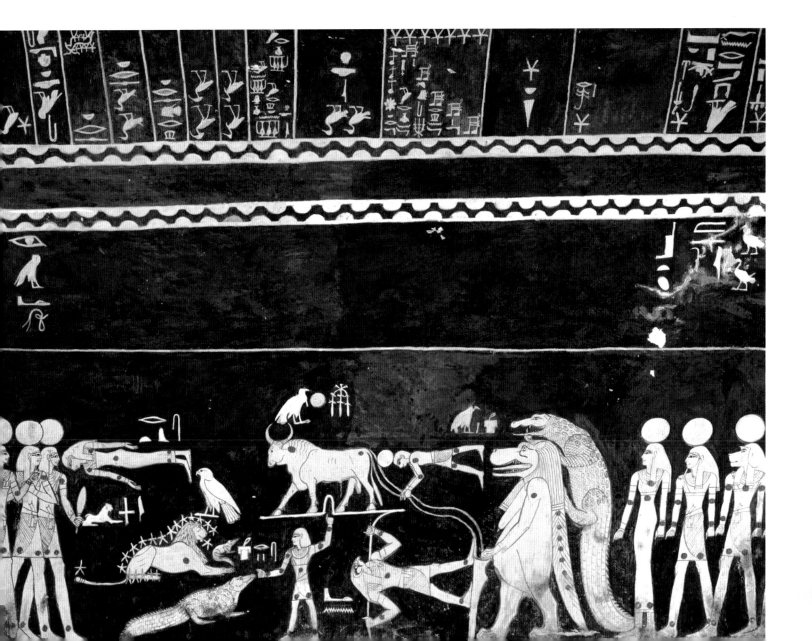

In the ancient Egyptians' calendar, New Year's Day fell on 15 July and was heralded by the reappearance, after an absence of 70 days, of the brightest star in the sky. Known by the Romans as Sirius – 'the sharp one' – because of its brilliance, its modern name is the Dog Star and it can be seen directly south of Orion's Belt. At about the time Sirius reappeared – a time known as Akhet (inundation) – the waters of the Nile would start to rise. As the river swelled, an area of 11,000 sq. km (4250 square miles) in the valley was transformed into a massive watery plain. The flooding river brought with it a black sediment which was rich in alluvial silt, a natural fertilizer.

Why the flood came in summer, rather than winter, was a question that perplexed the Greek historian Herodotus:

Above: Detail from the Tomb of Sennedjem in Luxor, showing the tomb owner and his wife ploughing and reaping wheat in the afterlife – a mirror of life along the banks of the Nile.

ANCIENT EGYPT

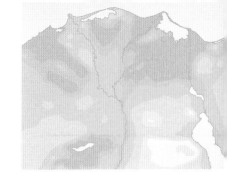

*As regards the nature of the river, neither from the priests nor yet from any other man was
I able to obtain any knowledge: and I was desirous especially to learn from them about these
matters, namely why the Nile comes down increasing in volume from the summer solstice
onwards for a hundred days, and then, when it has reached the number of these days,
turns and goes back, failing in its stream, so that through the whole winter season it continues
to be low, and until the summer solstice returns.*

But the Egyptians did not question what had always been; they were more concerned about
the level of the flood.

The yield of the harvest – and therefore the prosperity of the country – depended on the flood
and the silt it brought. Acutely conscious of this, the Egyptians placed Nilometers – stone
measuring devices – along the banks of the Nile at the southern end of the country. These
recorded the height of the water and helped to predict the level of the flood downstream. A rise
of about 7.5 m (25 feet) was expected. As the river rose, the entire nation was involved in
building elaborate systems of embankments, dykes, barriers, canals and basins to manage the
flow of the water.

In November the water began to recede, revealing land blackened and fertilized by sediment.
This time was called Peret (emergence) and was the season for planting and growing. The
blackened land became an ordered grid of fields, and was so fertile that the early farmers
needed only to put seeds in the ground and leave them to grow. However, as the population
increased, farming techniques became more sophisticated. Irrigation was employed on a larger
scale, aided by the *shaduf* – an extended arm with a swinging bucket that enabled water to be
transported from the river or canals to higher ground. This allowed a great variety of crops to be
grown: for example, barley, emmer wheat, fava beans, lentils, peas, lettuces, cucumbers,
onions, radishes and melons.

While the crops grew, the waters continued to recede, reaching their lowest point around
Shemu (harvest) in March. Thanks to the fertility of the land and the reliability of Egypt's weather,
harvests were generally plentiful – ancient Egyptians could proudly boast of 'granaries
approaching heaven, grain heaps like mountains'. It is not surprising they believed they were
blessed. So productive was the land that after the Roman conquest of Egypt in 30 BC the
country became known as the breadbasket of the empire.

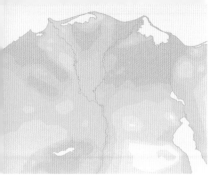

# A CENTRAL LIFELINE

All the inhabited land was within a few miles of the Nile, so nowhere and nobody was far from the river. Dynastic Egypt therefore had the best internal communications system of the ancient world, and this played an important part in the kingdom's cohesiveness and the longevity of its civilization. Supplies from each province were co-ordinated and delivered to vast storehouses at the national capital and distributed in times of need.

The Nile also provided the Egyptians with a means of transport. They became master boatbuilders and were good sailors – at least when navigating the river. Their early boats were made of reeds but later wood was used, particularly sycamore. This is notoriously difficult to work and must have required quite advanced woodworking skills. Simple and efficient triangular sails, similar to those on feluccas today, were invented in about 3350 BC, before the dynastic period.

Generally, it took about two weeks to travel downriver from Thebes to Memphis (roughly Luxor to Cairo) – a distance of 680 km (420 miles). Travelling upstream was slower, but boats could generally count on being helped by the prevailing northerly winds. Along the way the banks of the Nile were punctuated with harbours and artificial ports, which allowed goods to be distributed throughout the country. Of course, during the flood, boats could reach almost every corner of the flood plain. This was important for the delivery of the millions of tonnes of granite used in tombs and the great temple complexes. Much of the granite was mined from quarries at Aswan, a full 240 km (150 miles) from Luxor alone. It could never have been transported such distances without the Nile's help.

# THE FERTILE VALLEY

Acting like a giant oasis set in the middle of the desert, the Nile concentrated wildlife. Pied kingfishers hovered over the river, waiting to catch fish rising to the surface, their black and white wings a dazzling stroboscope. As boats plied up and down the river, sailors would have seen Nile crocodiles emerging from the water to warm themselves in the sun. These giant reptiles laid their eggs at the onset of the inundation so that their young would hatch while there were still pools in which to hunt frogs and toads, safely out of reach of the giant Nile perch. Fish were plentiful and easy to catch. During the flood, catfish migrated to the shallow pools of the flood plain to breed and fishermen would also have known the tilapia, a fish that broods its young in its mouth, appearing to give birth to live offspring.

**Above left:** The pied kingfisher hunts its prey by hovering over water. Its call – a high-pitched 'kwik kwik kwik' – is frequently heard along the Nile.

**Above right:** The ancient Egyptians considered crocodiles so sacred that sanctuaries were built to honour them, where they were given ceremonial offerings. When they died they were mummified.

In the Nile's muddy beds, gallinule (or purple swamp hens) would have been seen using their extraordinary oversized feet to hold papyrus stems for eating. The mud itself provided homes not only for swallows, who built their nests from it, but also for people who used mud bricks to build their houses. Hippos patrolled the margins of the river, a continual threat to people and their crops. Out on the fields, scarab beetles rolled balls of cattle dung – their unlikely cargo an incubation chamber for their young. (Once buried in the ground, the young could safely feed and grow in their subterranean larder before emerging.) Meanwhile, farmers fought a continual battle against the rats and mice that attempted to rob their grain stores. It was here in Egypt that cats were domesticated in order to keep down the number of rodents.

Where the black land of the valley met the red land of the desert, hamadryas baboons gathered together at dusk in groups of over 700, chattering nervously as predators circled them. In the morning they sat upright, warming themselves, before dividing into small foraging parties to find acacia flowers and grass seeds to eat. Acacias were home to nesting birds such as hoopoes, the trees' spines protecting the nests from would-be egg-raiders like the mongoose. Their deep-set roots allowed them to endure partial drowning each year during the flood, while their tough, waxy leaves held moisture and protected them in the blazing heat.

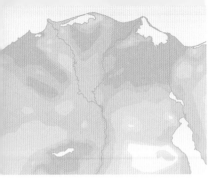

By day peregrine and lanner falcons exploited the skies to swoop on unsuspecting prey, whilst by night barn owls hunted silently. With their hunter-gatherer origins, the human inhabitants of the valley looked for prey too, their targets the various species that lived on the edge of the desert: hartebeest, deer, wild ass, hares, dorcas gazelle and oryx antelope. Larger animals were also drawn by the power of the river. In early dynastic times elephants, rhinos, lions, hyenas and giraffes roamed the valley. They were gradually hunted and pushed out as the civilization grew. In the desert itself there were scorpions and horned vipers that waited motionless, ready to ambush their prey. Under the baking sun, lappet-faced and Egyptian vultures scavenged carcasses, their feasting often rudely interrupted by jackal-like wild dogs.

The Nile was also a staging post on the migration corridor between Europe and Africa, and every year Egyptians would have witnessed the arrival and departure of flocks of birds in their thousands. Pintail ducks, Egyptian geese, flamingos, pelicans, storks and sacred ibis were some of the species that added to the colourful spectacle of life on the river.

**Above:** The scarab beetle is a symbol of good luck that has endured from ancient to modern times.

**Opposite:** Temple columns at Medinet Habu, Luxor. The inner workings of temples were unseen by ordinary people, but within them elaborate rituals were undertaken to help maintain the cosmic order.

Yet despite the fecundity of the Nile valley the entire civilization of ancient Egypt hinged on that one annual event: the flood. When the normal order prevailed and the flood was good, the Egyptians prospered. But they were hostages to fortune: if the flood was too weak or too strong they could perish. Knowing that they were vulnerable to natural events, they looked for a supernatural key to the order of their self-contained universe.

## TAMING CHAOS

Religion was central to the lives of the ancient Egyptians, so much so that Herodotus claimed that 'Egyptians are the most religious people on earth'. Our understanding of the beliefs of the pharaonic age comes mainly from the abundant literature found on the walls of temples and tombs, on sarcophagi and coffins and on the papyrus scrolls that have survived through the ages. Ironically, much of it was written for the spirits of the dead and was never intended to be seen again by the living. This literature is largely religious in nature, comprising hymns, ceremonies and charms. What it reveals is a surprisingly optimistic religion based on the

Right: The emergence of land from water was a fundamental event of the creation myth, and these triangular shapes that pointed heaven-wards were a possible inspiration for the pyramids. Lake Nasser is strewn with these 'primordial mounds'.

Opposite: Osiris, God of the Underworld, from the tomb of Ramesses I. His face is painted green to symbolize the renewal of life caused by the flooding of the Nile.

Overleaf: Isis (right) was the mythical sister/wife of Osiris, and mother of Horus. From the tomb of Horemheb.

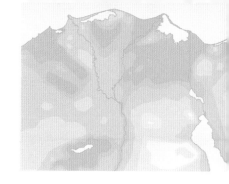

ancient Egyptians' sense that they lived in a land that was blessed by the gods. Ritual was of vital importance and a great number of different rites had to be performed in precise ways at specific times. And it was a religion that apparently involved a huge number of deities.

At the heart of the belief system was the idea that the world was created out of chaos (*isfet*) and that order (*ma'at*) was maintained only with great difficulty by the intervention of the gods. The Egyptians saw all around them evidence of the fundamental tension between these forces – the daily rising of the sun and the seasonal emergence of the land from the Nile's flood were both interpreted as the re-establishment of order from chaos.

The most widespread of their creation myths told that there was one god of creation, the source of all elements and forces. They attempted to name this profoundly inexplicable entity as Atum, Re or Ptah, but ultimately concluded, 'He is too great to investigate, too powerful to know'. Atum appeared on an island that emerged from the dark, watery world of chaos, like the islands that emerged from the receding waters of the Nile flood. He then created, or evolved into, all life. To explain this idea the Egyptians used the metaphor of birth. Atum generated Shu (the void) and Tefnut, his female partner. This pair engendered Geb (the earth) and Nut (the sky), who in turn gave birth to Osiris, Isis, Seth and Nephthys who represented the different forces of life and sexuality.

Osiris was the god most closely associated with the Nile, and the myth of Osiris and Isis was central to the religious belief – and observance – of the ancient Egyptians. Osiris ruled Egypt with his sister-wife Isis. (Marrying siblings was considered normal practice because it maintained sacred bloodlines.) Isis discovered wheat and barley, and Osiris taught his people how to cultivate them. But their brother Seth, associated with the forces of chaos or evil, was jealous. He murdered Osiris by cutting him into pieces, which he scattered all over the land. Isis found the pieces and bound them together, mummy-like. Her breath magically brought Osiris back to life, just long enough for them to conceive a son: Horus. Osiris became king of the underworld, where he ordained the Nile flood and its life-giving waters. Seth tried repeatedly to

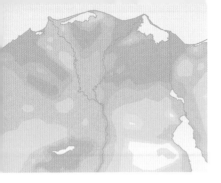

kill Horus but, though wounded, the child was protected and healed by his mother Isis. When he reached adulthood Horus continued to wrestle with Seth for the vacant throne of Osiris, ultimately emerging victorious.

Osiris was thus associated with the inundation and the crops that grew as a result, this regeneration of life being a part of the universal order. Images of the god show his face painted green to symbolize the fertility of the land. Seth was associated with tempestuous forces whose power, if untamed, would destroy the order of the world. Horus, meanwhile, was the crucial link between the real and supernatural worlds. He had to avenge his father's murder and maintain the natural order by taming Seth's chaos. In the eyes of the Egyptians he was associated with the sun and personified by the pharaoh.

The ancient Egyptians saw the myth of Osiris and Isis and the principle of *ma'at* – the control of opposing forces – in each 24-hour cycle. The dying sun, as it made its journey into the Duat, encountered a giant serpent that patrolled the underworld. The chaotic, coiling creature tried to

**Below:** The sacred ibis uses its long curved beak to probe for crustaceans, snails and aquatic insects in the mud. So revered were they that killing one, whether accidental or not, was punishable by death.

sabotage the sun's journey at the doors to each of the night's 12 'rooms'. In the middle of the night, however, the sun came across the body of Osiris. At this point the sun and Osiris became one. Given new life by Osiris, the sun could proceed through the remainder of the night towards rebirth at dawn.

The yearly cycle of life on the Nile was also interpreted as a struggle between order and chaos, between Osiris and Seth. During the harvest, the farmers' sickles and threshing 'broke' the wheat and barley. This was reminiscent of Seth murdering Osiris and cutting him into pieces. The star Sirius, which heralded the New Year, was interpreted as the goddess Isis returning to search for her dead husband Osiris. It was said that as the Nile started to swell, her tears nourished the waters to help them to rise. But the flood was a time when Seth could disrupt order – too much or too little water could cause devastation. To tame the power of the rising waters the pharaoh, personifying Horus, would ceremonially dig the first irrigation channel. Once the waters had receded, the farmers sowed their crops – this was seen as the pieces of Osiris's mutilated body being scattered over the land by Seth. There were tales of ritualistic weeping as the seeds were sown. But as the months progressed, the crops grew again in the fertile soil, just as Osiris had been

Above: The peregrine falcon was believed to be god of the skies and the living image of Horus. It was closely identified with the pharaoh.

brought back to life by Isis. A hymn was sung: 'Osiris! You went away, but you have returned, you fell asleep, but you have awakened, you died, but you live again.' As the crops grew and Osiris rose again each year Egypt was blessed with a surplus that ensured the strength of the nation.

The pharaoh, as the personification of Horus, was ultimately responsible for the success or failure of the flood, and, as the god, he was portrayed as a falcon, a king of the sky, able to survey everything in his kingdom. The all-seeing eye of Horus was a common image throughout the kingdom. He was also associated with the cobra and the vulture, the emblems

**Above:** The ancient Egyptian name for the cobra meant 'she who stands up'. The cobra's venom glands are modified salivary glands, and venom is either injected into prey or spat out in defence.

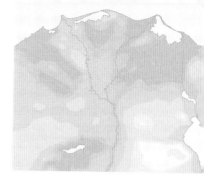

of the two lands that had been united to form Egypt. The cobra represented Lower Egypt and was known as the 'pharaoh's protector' – when one of these snakes is disturbed it rears up and extends its neck muscles to create the classic 'cobra' shape, a threat posture that makes it look bigger than it really is. The lappet-faced vulture was the symbol of Upper Egypt. In the searing heat of the Nile valley these birds stand near carcasses, with their wings outstretched to nearly 3 m (10 feet) to help regulate their body temperature. The Egyptians believed these formidable-looking creatures were protecting the carcass, their prize. In contrast to the pharaoh, the wicked Seth was rarely associated with known animals. He was more usually portrayed as a chimerical beast that represented the anarchic forces of nature.

Above: The powerful hooked bill of the lappet-faced vulture cuts easily into carrion. It uses its bulk and outstretched wings to chase other birds off and so dominate the kill.

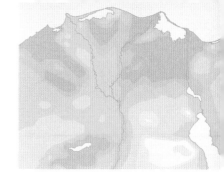

Over the course of the Egyptian civilization Osiris, Isis and Horus were joined by a multitude of other gods, many of whom were also represented as animals. Crocodiles were believed to have emerged out of the primordial waters from which the world had been created to help banish chaos, and were worshipped as the god Sobek – in whom the elements of the sun, earth and water were united. The flocks of ibis that arrived at the start of the flood were thought to have divine knowledge and these sacred birds became Thoth, the god of writing and all intellectual activity. The hippos that defended their young so aggressively became Tauert, the goddess of childbirth. The formidable bull was seen as an earthly manifestation of divine power – a sacred 'Apis' bull was selected to lead a sumptuous life surrounded by doting priests. The Greeks and Romans, whose gods were essentially human, found the Egyptians' vast menagerie of divinities extraordinary.

The symbolism of the natural world extended beyond the portrayal of gods. It was believed that frogs and toads reproduced spontaneously, so their 'autogenesis' became a symbol of birth and resurrection. Frog amulets were popular gifts at New Year. The troupes of hamadryas baboons that chattered excitedly at sunrise were thought to be sun worshippers. The diminutive scarab beetle, rolling its ball of dung, was associated with the solar cycle: the burying of the dung ball was sunset and death, and the emergence of the young from the buried ball was sunrise and rebirth. Scarabs became popular good luck charms. During the night, as the sun made its journey underground, catfish helped to guide it through the darkness. The inherent power of all animals was recognized. If they were considered malignant, worship helped to appease some of their more dangerous tendencies. If they were sacred, they could not be killed on pain of death.

# RITUALS AND CUSTOMS

The ancient Egyptians believed it was rituals that helped to maintain the balance between order and chaos. Their world and universe were perfect at the time of creation, but threatened by chaos. Thus their temples were models of a perfect universe: the floors represented the river; the stone columns, papyrus reeds; and the ceilings, decorated with stars, the sky above. The constant repetition of rituals was necessary to maintain the state of perfection, to ward off chaos or *isfet*. Generally these rituals involved propitiating, through offerings, the gods who controlled the forces of the world. At the heart of the sacred rites was the pharaoh, much of whose life was spent performing in a giant theatre of ritual where each word, each action and each ablution was a vital element in the taming of chaos by order. It was a monumental responsibility, but even when the pharaoh died his role continued.

Opposite: Hamadryas baboons were an everyday presence in ancient Egypt. Females were often adopted as pets, but the males could be particularly aggressive. The hieroglyphic 'to be furious' was represented by the image of an angry baboon.

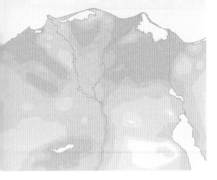

Because so much of our knowledge of the ancient Egyptians comes from the art and literature found in tombs their civilization is commonly perceived as one obsessed with death. But it could equally be seen as one obsessed with life. The Egyptians tended to see the afterworld as a mirror of the world they lived in, and tombs were generally stocked and decorated in such a way that the dead could continue to enjoy the same luxuries in death as they had enjoyed in life.

The burial customs of the ancient Egyptians were built on the traditions of the predynastic peoples of Upper Egypt, who observed that bodies buried in the dry sand on the edge of the desert did not decay. They developed a belief that individuals did not really 'die', and death came to be seen as a transition to another stage of existence. It followed, in the minds of these peoples, that if the deceased were going on a journey they would need provisions and some possessions, and tombs started to be elaborately stocked. Nowhere is this more apparent than at the predynastic town of Naqada, just north of Luxor. Here thousands of graves have been excavated revealing that, even before 4000 BC, people were buried with provisions for the afterlife. The tombs also contain stone jars decorated with animals – artefacts destined to last for eternity. These are a testament to another significant achievement of the people of Naqada: their skill at working hard stone, such as basalt and granite, that was available to them in Upper Egypt.

As funerary beliefs evolved, the Egyptians became less inclined to leave the preservation of the body to chance or nature, and mummification became an essential component of the burial ritual. The vital organs of the deceased were removed and stored in jars, and the body was dehydrated using natron, then anointed with oils and resin, and wrapped in cloth to maintain its shape. Behind this practice was the belief that the spirit could travel around by day but needed to return to the body each night. If the body were destroyed, the spirit would search for it in vain for eternity; if the body were preserved, the spirit could become immortal. As is so often the case, the actions of humans reflected elements of the myth of Osiris and Isis: the broken body of Osiris was bound together and preserved by Isis. She was aided by a dog-headed god called Anubis, derived from the jackal-like creatures that scavenged around graveyards.

When burying pharaohs and other noblemen the Egyptians tried to ensure that in the afterlife their spirits could enjoy not only the same foods they had enjoyed during their mortal lives, but also the same luxuries and diversions. They placed real and symbolic objects – or representations of objects – in the tombs, a practice that evolved continually through the dynasties. In the Old Kingdom (c.2525–2130 BC) models of servants were sometimes buried with the dead – by magical means they could 'serve' the deceased for eternity. By the Middle Kingdom (c.1980–1630 BC) the tomb might be stocked with elaborate models of granaries,

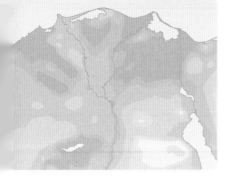

ships and workshops, all complete with model workers, so that the deceased could enjoy the produce. Later, the walls of tombs were decorated with scenes of farming, fishing, hunting, the harvest, birds, animals, papyrus swamps, boats, the Nile itself – all depicted with great precision and clarity so that they could be recognized and used by the spirit. Beds of corn in the shape of Osiris – 'Osiris beds' – were sometimes placed in tombs where they would grow, symbolizing the continuation of life. Originally, only the pharaoh received such treatment but from the late Old Kingdom onwards the promise of eternal life with Osiris extended to all his subjects.

By the time of the New Kingdom (c.1539–1075 BC) the construction, adornment and stocking of tombs reached its zenith. This was a major industry, and the burial of the dead was a highly ritualized procedure. The most important tombs were, of course, those of the pharaohs and thousands of people might have been employed preparing them in the burial chambers of the Valley of the Kings. At times the banks of the Nile probably resembled one large construction site as successive pharaohs competed with their predecessors, building ever more extravagant structures. But while their tombs were to some extent designed to reflect their greatness, they were not only monuments. It was vital to the order and prosperity of Egypt that a dead pharaoh should proceed to the afterlife to join Osiris. And as the journey was a perilous one, images and literature were often placed in the tombs to help him find his way.

A pharaoh's burial ceremony involved a series of precise rituals that would assist his spirit on its journey – a journey so complex that there were funerary maps and texts to guide it to the afterlife. The Pyramid Texts (found on the walls of early tombs), the Coffin Texts (found on coffins and sarcophagi in later tombs), and *The Book of the Dead* (written on papyrus scrolls in the New Kingdom period) served this purpose.

The Egyptians believed that when the pharaoh's spirit left his body it wandered through the underworld in search of Osiris in his hall of judgement. There were 12 stages to the journey – one for each hour of the night. At each stage the spirit was asked a series of questions by hostile doorkeepers – failure to answer correctly meant destruction. If the spirit passed the tests and arrived at the hall of judgement, it was ushered into the presence of Osiris, where it had to endure the hardest test of all: the weighing of the heart, which was thought to be the centre of thought, memory and personality. The heart had to be in balance with a feather, which represented *ma'at* – order and justice – and was weighed by Anubis. Ibis-headed Thoth recorded the verdict. If the heart failed to balance, the spirit faced annihilation by Ammut, a terrifying hybrid of crocodile, lion and hippo, who crouched by the scales. If the heart was in

Left: Mummy mask of
Tuya, the mother of Queen
Tiye and grandmother of
Akhenaten. Tuya was
buried with her husband
Yuya at Luxor.

Overleaf: The Valley of
the Kings at Luxor. For
thousands of years this
barren valley has been
the home of the dead,
and a sharp contrast to
the fertile strip and life-
giving water at its feet.

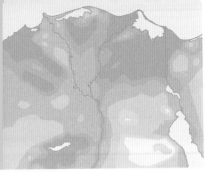

balance with *ma'at* the spirit could join the realm of Osiris and embark on the sun's boat as it made its nightly journey. At the tenth hour of the night, the sun and the spirit were met by a scarab beetle who would help to push them towards their rebirth at dawn. (A stone scarab, its underside inscribed with charms, was sometimes placed over the deceased's chest to assist their spirit through the ordeal.) Finally, as the morning sky began to glow, the sun and the pharaoh rose triumphantly, together with the hawk-headed god Horus. The dead pharaoh was now part of both the annual regeneration of Osiris and the daily renewal of the sun.

# THE DEATH OF ANCIENT EGYPT

Despite all the rituals designed to maintain order, the chaos of Seth sometimes gained the ascendancy over the combined power of Horus, Osiris and Isis. The Bible tells of catastrophes such as plagues of locusts that decimated crops – tales that are probably echoes of real events. And the Nile, despite being one of the most reliable river systems on earth, could itself be a victim of the vagaries of nature: records show that the flood sometimes failed several years in a row. These prolonged droughts would have depleted food stores and caused widespread starvation. In addition, sustained periods of overflooding would have been equally damaging to the harvest. Recent scientific evidence has linked these extended periods of 'chaos' – which would have undermined the government of dynastic Egypt – to periods of climatic change resulting from an ancient El Niño.

In the midst of natural disasters, whether these were the result of the flood failing or of overflooding, the Egyptians' religious faith must have been sorely tested. However, it is more likely that their rituals gained in gravitas at these times. After all, these rituals had helped to guarantee the cycles of renewal that had allowed their civilization to come into being and survive for thousands of years. This traditionalism was understandable but it would ultimately lead to the civilization's demise.

Religious belief in ancient Egypt revolved around the idea that the world was perfect when it was created, and there was a profound mistrust of change. The pharaoh Akhenaten, who ruled from *c*.1353–1336 BC, was considered a heretic by his successors due to his revolutionary idea of abandoning the complex array of gods in favour of just one (the world's first monotheistic religion) and loosening the rigid style of art in favour of more humanistic forms. The majority of the images and artefacts from his extraordinarily dynamic and radical reign were destroyed soon after his death, and there was a dramatic return to 'old' values when Tutankhamun succeeded him.

**Opposite:** Akhenaten worshipping the sun god. A roofless sanctuary at his temple complex received the sun's rays, which are depicted here delivering the ankh, symbol of life.

During the New Kingdom period Egypt's empire had become vast, stretching from Nubia to Syria. But despite the Egyptians' power and wealth they were ultimately inward-looking. The centre of their world was the Nile. Rather than look forward, they drew their strength from their past and from their vision of creation. But the world was changing around them, and this insular and conservative civilization eventually began to look outdated and out of touch. Even as basic and practical a technology as the wheeled chariot arrived 1000 years after it had been adopted in Mesopotamia.

Egyptians embraced the power of civilization, but they were anchored to the repetitive rhythms of their culture – the cycles of renewal and regeneration. Perhaps the reasons for the country's conflicting nature were there from the very start, when the two rival kingdoms of Egypt became one nation in about 3000 BC. The valley people of Upper Egypt, with their strong religious and cultural identity, effectively subsumed the farming people in the delta of Lower Egypt. But the world that had seemed so contained when the kingdom of Egypt was formed eventually evolved into one of several powerful, competing empires. In the eighth and seventh centuries BC Egypt was ruled by the Kushites, its neighbours to the south, and in 332 BC it fell to the Greeks. Three hundred years later, in 30 BC, it was conquered by the Romans. The country was demoted to the role of breadbasket for the Roman Empire, while its pharaonic culture was steadily erased, and finally eradicated with the adoption of Christianity.

The Nile had witnessed mankind feeling its way out of the fog of the prehistoric era and emerging triumphantly from the Neolithic revolution. It had given birth to the world's first great state and great civilization. Yet the ordered universe the ancient Egyptians created and attempted to maintain was ultimately just an illusion. Their knowledge extended only as far as the perimeter of the universe they had conceived. Within this universe they knew exactly what the Nile did, and they imagined magnificent scenarios to explain its forces. But they never sought the real reasons for the Nile's behaviour – the true source of its power. Perhaps it was because they believed they had all the answers they needed, answers that had served them well for so long. Or maybe it was because the real reasons for the Nile's power lay further upstream, outside their ordered universe, in the chaos beyond.

CHAPTER 2

# THE GREAT
# FLOOD

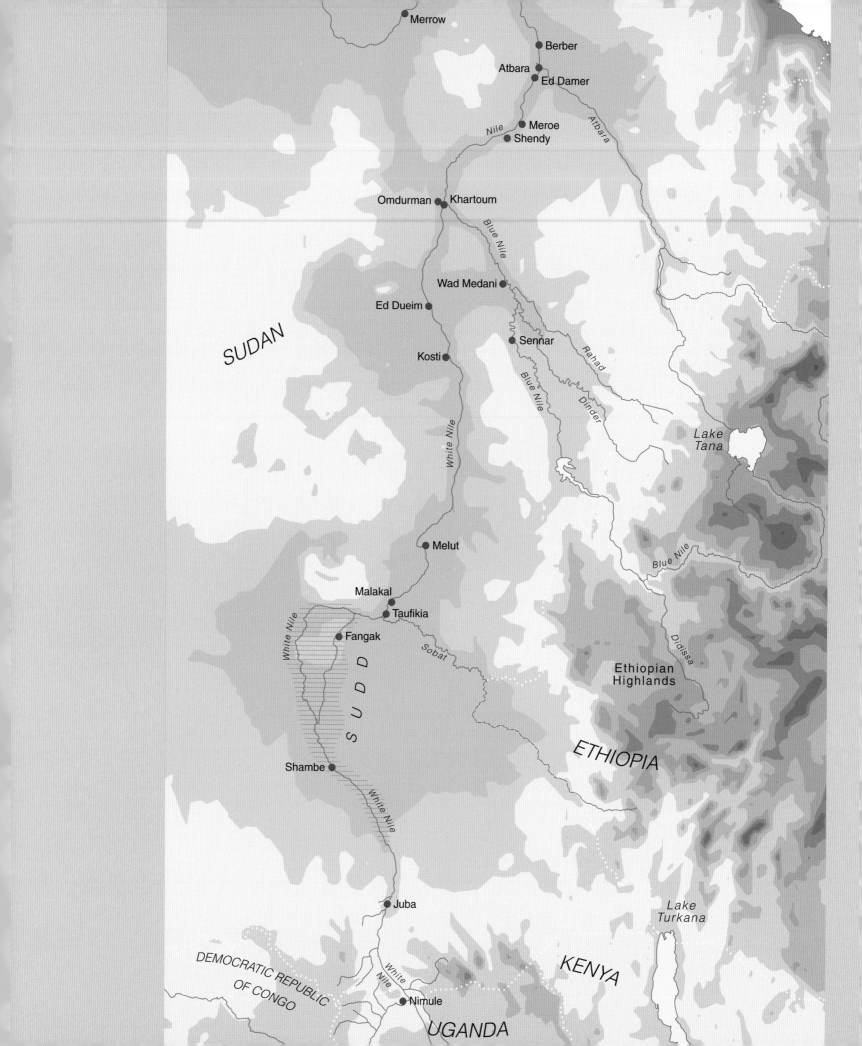

**Above:** As the Nile cuts through the deserts of northern Sudan it waters a belt of fertile land only a few fields wide.

The power of the pyramid-building pharaohs came from the fertility of the Nile. But the river also distributed its gifts much further south, hundreds of miles upstream in Nubia, an area now part of northern Sudan. Here, too, the Nile dominated the landscape – an axis of Eden cutting a green swathe through a forbidding desert known to the Arabs as 'the belly of stones'. Even in present-day northern Sudan, people still cling to a 100-m (330-foot)-wide strip of irrigated land on the Nile's banks.

In Nubia, too, the Nile gave birth to a pyramid-building civilization. Some 2400 km (1500 miles) from the river's mouth, on a rocky plateau sitting among soft, wind-sculpted sand dunes, a line of distinctively tall, thin pyramids stands guard over the Nile valley and the ruins of the royal city of Meroe, the capital of the kingdom of Kush. This was another great empire, culturally distinct from ancient Egypt. As in Egypt, the Nile had provided natural riches in such excess that it allowed the Kushites the luxury of building imposing tombs for their pharaohs and queens. As

well as surplus food, the Nile provided trees – fuel to smelt enough iron from the surrounding rocks to make the Kushites an important regional power.

It has been estimated that the dark-skinned peoples of Nubia inhabited this area as early as 8000 BC – long before the birth of ancient Egypt. The Kushite 'black pharaohs' ruled Nubia from the ninth to the fourth century BC. Although there was much interchange with the civilization of Egypt to the north, the Kushites maintained a distinct culture of their own. But it is less well understood: they left fewer records and, unlike the hieroglyphics of the Egyptians, the meaning of their written language has still not been deciphered. We know they conquered Egypt in about 750 BC, at which point they controlled almost a quarter of Africa, but this powerful civilization remains an enigma.

Below: The pyramid-builders of the Nubian kingdom of Kush, now northern Sudan, left behind few clues as to their unique culture and language. The pyramids at Meroe are great enigmas and represent a key frontier of modern archaeology.

Although the Nile was an obvious navigation route, the ancient Egyptians never managed to travel far upstream. They were foiled by a set of six dangerous cataracts, or rapids, that started after Aswan and made the river unnavigable. So their knowledge of the Nile to the south and, crucially, the source of the great flood on which they depended, was based on second-hand accounts from neighbours such as the Kushites. Even in Roman times, when the glory of ancient Egypt began to fade, the Nile's great secret remained intact.

It was the introduction of the camel to Africa by the Persian conquerors of Egypt from about AD 200 that heralded a change. As the continent began to open up to trade, Nubia became criss-crossed by camel caravan routes across the desert. The Kushites, strategically based on the Nile at Meroe, initially benefited from this traffic but Africa's growing accessibility was eventually to be their undoing. A succession of invading armies came up the river or down from the mountains in search of slaves, gold and ivory. By AD 350, the kingdom of Kush had fallen to a trading rival from Ethiopia – the Christian state of Axum – and the Kushite culture was lost. But while wave after wave of invasion changed the human landscape, the Nile kept flowing and flooding, just as constant and enigmatic as ever.

After the fall of Meroe the nearby bankside town of Shendy took on the role of thriving market and meeting place for over 1000 years. Like Meroe, it was well positioned on the great river, at its closest point to the Red Sea, and straddled the caravan routes of the Sahara. Arab traders

from the west, slave raiders from the north and pilgrims heading for Mecca to the east all passed through the town.

A little upstream from Shendy and the pyramids at Meroe the Nile splits in two. Here lies the city that has become the new hub of the region: vibrant, bustling Khartoum, the capital of Sudan. Khartoum is one of Africa's great crossroads – the meeting place for an enormous variety of peoples from thousands of miles around.

The city owes its importance to the Arabs. By the fifteenth century AD Arab Muslims had infiltrated Nubia, usurping Christian kingdoms that had developed after the fall of the Kushites. Military invasions, trade and intermarriage led to domination by the Muslim faith and the Arabic

THE GREAT FLOOD

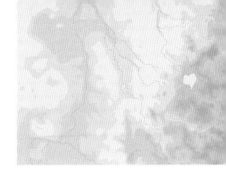

language. In the early 1820s, Mohammed Ali, the Turkish Viceroy of Egypt, sent an Egyptian invasion force into what is now Sudan. By 1824, he had moved the centre of commerce from Shendy upstream to Khartoum, where he could control movements up and down both forks of the Nile to the south. The commercial stakes were high. Khartoum had a booming agricultural industry, and trade was feverish: by 1850 some 50,000 slaves worth £250,000 (the equivalent of £13 million in today's money), and ivory worth £40,000 (the equivalent of £2 million), flowed out of the south every year.

Khartoum today maintains its status as a vibrant hub for large swathes of Africa. Goods still flow out of the deserts to the west, via Khartoum to the Red Sea. People still take months to walk their cattle to market, and merchants from the Middle East still come to the city to buy camels. As capital of Africa's largest country, itself home to 597 tribes and 134 languages, Khartoum is a unique melting pot. The centre of town is a human kaleidoscope of colours, religions and tribes. Arabia meets Africa and east meets west.

Islam has remained dominant here, with Arabic its voice. A diverse Muslim community still supports many old traditions. Every Friday, just before sunset, Sufis – Islamic mystics and respected elders – gather in front of a brightly decorated tomb, often dressed in rich technicolour gowns. Drums resonate like an ancient heartbeat as the expectant crowd that encircles them begins a rhythmic chant of '*La ilaha illa Allah*' (No God but Allah). The rhythmic chanting synchronizes and intensifies. The Sufis begin to spin with arms outstretched, fixed with the most distant of stares as they are urged into a trance by the increasingly feverish prayer of the crowd. One cannot fail to be swept away by the intensity of the spectacle – the noise, the rhythm, the dust and the magical smell of frankincense. These are the 'whirling dervishes' of Sudan. Their mesmeric dance at this fork in the Nile is a living memory of a ritual from Islam's earliest days here. At the height of their trance, the Sufis believe that their souls are communicating with Allah, being cleansed of evil, while only their physical body is visible to the crowd. For minutes at a time they spin, consumed by their calling, some collapsing into the dust. The spell is finally

Below: A chanting crowd urges a Sufi into a spinning trance. These Islamic mystics, sometimes known as 'whirling dervishes', believe that this altered state allows them to reach out to Allah, spanning the divide between heaven and earth.

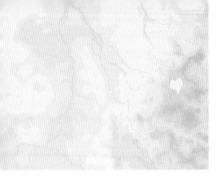

broken by the sunset call to prayer from the nearby mosque, singing out over the excited hubbub. Prayers are offered, and the crowd disperses into the dusty city.

The Nile dominates Khartoum. Crops still arrive in the city's markets from its verdant flood plain, and the noisy, bank-side fish market demonstrates that the river itself is still a reliable source of food. It seems impervious to change and remains somewhat untamed – when the floods are unusually high they can still devastate parts of the city. Such a disaster occurred as recently as 1988.

In the centre of Khartoum the two rivers, the Blue Nile and the White Nile, meet in what Arab poetry has described as 'the longest kiss in history'. Out of the flood season, where the two waters come together but run parallel without mixing for a few hundred metres, it is possible to see why the two arms have different names: the Blue Nile is more a brownish-green than blue, and the White Nile a paler brownish-grey. This difference in colour hints at very different beginnings and personalities for the two arms, but offers few clues as to which bears the greatest gift. In the dry season the Blue Nile flows clear but narrow from Ethiopia in the southeast, while the White Nile, flowing wide and muddy from the south, seems to be the more significant.

**Below:** Even in modern times a larger than average Nile flood can still cause devastation, as happened in Khartoum in 1988.

Left: At Khartoum the Blue Nile (left) and the White Nile (right) meet in what Arab poetry has described as 'the longest kiss in history'.

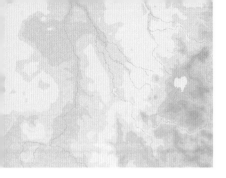

# THE WHITE NILE

Heading up the White Nile it is not long before one arrives at one of Africa's best-kept secrets. As the desert is left behind, the land gradually turns green. Seas of sand become seas of reeds so large that they sweep to a flat horizon in every direction. This is arguably the largest swamp in the world: 600 km (370 miles) long, covering up to 32,000 sq. km (12,355 square miles), with silt and marsh sediments thought to be up to an astonishing 10 km (6 miles) deep. All around, the view is dominated by papyrus, the 'paper reed', whose distinctive feathery flower heads tower 4 m (13 feet) above the water. Lush water plants crowd at the reeds' ankles, knitting a dense green fabric. It is a far cry from the deserts of the north.

But this is no oasis paradise. This enigmatic water-world is called the Sudd, from the Arabic for 'obstacle'. Not only does it present an enormous contorted maze of papyrus stands and waterways to the human explorer, but it is constantly changing. The many air spaces in papyrus stems give the reeds great buoyancy. They form huge floating rafts, called 'sudds', which are dense enough to support the weight of an elephant. These break free and drift like huge, apple-green icebergs, often blocking waterways when they finally come to rest again, knitting back into the marshes' dense fabric. Through this green maze winds the White Nile, its edges constantly challenged and redefined by the restless sudds.

Despite the frenetic human activity up the Nile to Khartoum, the Sudd remained unchanged and unexplored for thousands of years. In AD 61 the Romans were driven back by this seemingly impenetrable swamp and its reputation as a timeless wilderness held firm until Turko–Egyptian slave traders finally managed to cross it in 1840. The Victorian explorer Samuel Baker followed in 1862, and described the swamp as 'heaven for mosquitoes, damp hell for man'.

Even today, the Sudd remains a formidable place in which to live or explore, and a barrier to invasion or influence from the north. In the twentieth century it became the stage for the age-old feud between an Islamic world to the north and a Christian or animist world to the south. Sudan's legacy of the slave trade, and now a struggle for control of the Sudd's 3 billion barrels of low-sulphur crude oil and its significant resources of water and fertile soil, have fuelled one of the world's longest civil wars. In the last 20 years alone, hundreds of thousands of people have been killed or displaced.

Below: Papyrus
dominates the labyrinthine
swamps of southern
Sudan. The plant's
buoyant stems allow it to
form huge floating rafts.

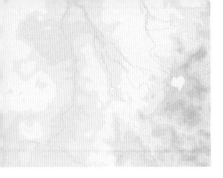

As few scientists have dared to visit the Sudd in recent years, we can only guess at how the Nile's great swamp has been affected by this latest sad chapter in its long history. Paradoxically, the war may have resulted in a stay of execution for the swamp itself. Work has stopped on a canal – 360 km (225 miles) long – through the Sudd, which would divert water for irrigation and hydroelectric projects downstream in northern Sudan and Egypt, but would drain large areas of the marsh, reducing it by nearly half. Were the scheme to be completed, the Sudd would be changed for ever and the way of life of many people who live there would be threatened.

## LIVING WITH THE SUDD

Despite the inhospitable climate, the Sudd's marshes are well populated, mostly by Dinka and Nuer people. These imposingly tall, slim, jet-black-skinned people of the Nile have a long tradition of cattle-breeding and a reputation for collective pride and defiance. It is thought that they have grazed their huge herds of cattle at the edge of the White Nile's marshes since the time of the ancient Egyptians, enduring the heat, the humidity and the ravages of mosquitoes and tick-borne disease. This is no tiny pocket of humanity lost in the wilderness: these people number over a million and represent one of the largest ethnic groups in Africa.

The age-old survival strategy of the Dinka and Nuer is to ebb and flow with the rhythms of the restless swamp. Always kept on the move, and with only wood and mud as building materials, they have never built great cities, monuments or tombs like those found in Egypt or Nubia. Instead, largely sheltered from outside influence by the protective barrier of the Sudd, their culture and way of life have been vigorously upheld by a long and complex tradition of symbols, stories and songs. Far from seeing the swamp as 'damp hell for man', the Dinka and Nuer firmly believe that their world is the best the earth can offer. They share a strong belief in spirits within nature, with the sky, the earth and the ebb and flow of river, rain and flood at the heart of their belief. Many wild animals, from lions to lizards and from crocodiles to crows, are associated with spirits or symbolic totems. This spiritual respect for the natural world has arisen for good reason. Whereas in the north the managed irrigation and neat fields show the strength of man's influence over the river, here the world of the Nile remains wild and fickle. Attempting to impose the same level of control would be an act of sheer folly.

The abundance and dominance of nature in the Sudd is recognized in Arab names for the three arms of the great river which define the swamp: 'Bahr el Zeraf' (river of the giraffes), 'Bahr el Ghazal' (river of the gazelles) and 'Bahr el Jebel' (river of the mountains). The marshes and flood

plains of the Sudd indeed support a rich fauna, including over 400 species of bird and more than 90 species of mammal, including some of the greatest concentrations of large mammals on earth. The rivers, lakes and marshes teem with fish. And there are mosquitoes in abundance: 63 species have been named so far and there are doubtless many more to be identified.

In the dry season, which peaks from January to March, all life crowds around the river channels and permanent marshes. The Nile's flood plain is packed with tiang – unusual-looking, long-faced, black and tan animals related to the wildebeest, which form herds several thousand strong. These are joined by similarly impressive numbers of diminutive mongalla gazelles. Estimates made before the current civil war suggested that up to a third of a million animals used the Nile as a dry-season refuge.

Above: The spotted-necked otter is poorly adapted for walking on land and spends most of its time in the water, only leaving it to eat and sleep.

THE GREAT FLOOD

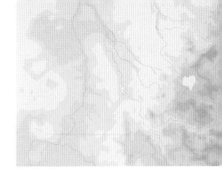

An even greater natural spectacle can be seen on the banks of the Pibor and Akobo rivers, tributaries of the White Nile to the east. White-eared kob – striking brown, black and white antelopes with large curved horns – gather in their tens of thousands. Some pre-war estimates put the total population at over a million – enough to rival the great herds on the Serengeti plain in Tanzania. Yet few outside the Sudd have even heard of the white-eared kob, such is the region's ability to keep so much hidden. In the dry season, diminishing supplies of fresh grass squeeze the kob into one of the greatest concentrations of large mammals on earth – an amazing 1000 animals per square kilometre (less than half a square mile).

The dry season is mating time for the kob, and overcrowding has led to the evolution of unusual courtship habits. Like many other mammals, the males set up territories and compete fiercely for the best sites in an attempt to attract females. But because the kob are packed together in such huge densities, the males' territories are tiny and often merely symbolic as they have no food value at all. Male aggression has become ritualized into posturing, signalling and the clashing of horns. It is more a board game than a pitched battle – a phenomenon known as lekking. Within each lek, 20 to 200 males perform, each defending his own tiny stage.

The Dinka and Nuer are also packed tightly along the edges of the river channels and marshes in the dry season. Many leave their permanent villages for the duration, and in each temporary camp several hundred people look after many thousand cattle. It is one of the most impressive and unusual gatherings of human beings and animals in the world. Tall, dark and striking young men, wearing little more than a ghost-like covering of ash, walk silhouetted through clouds of smoke and dust. With remarkable tenderness, they attend magnificent, scimitar-horned cattle, rubbing ash into their skin, polishing their horns and singing songs to them. The Dinka and Nuer are as close to their animals as any tribes on earth. The cow is the key to their survival in this unforgiving place and plays a powerful role in both their material and spiritual worlds. Milk, and sometimes blood, forms much of their diet. The dung is constantly burnt, the smoke and ash enshrouding man and beast alike in a ghostly deterrent to mosquitoes. A Dinka's cattle are rarely killed and eaten. They are more valuable alive, as a symbol of wealth, status and influence.

But impressive as these huge congregations of people, cattle and wild animals are, they raise a question. How can such a small area sustain such huge numbers year-round? The grazing is poor and diminishing, yet a million white-eared kob are gearing up to breed. It does not add up. At the very end of the dry season the Dinka and Nuer pack up camp and return to their villages, where they will raise a rapid crop of groundnuts, okra and sorghum. This can only mean one thing: the flood is coming.

**Opposite:** A Dinka man sings songs in praise of his prize bull – testimony to an age-old relationship that is both practical and spiritual.

**Overleaf:** Dry-season cattle camps are an integral part of the nomadic cycle of the Dinka's year. The ubiquitous shroud of smoke from burning cow dung serves as an insect repellent for man and beast alike.

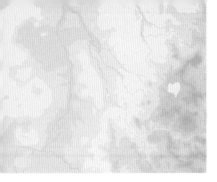

# LIVING WITH THE RAINS

April sees the start of the rains – a series of brief, torrential showers that last through to October. These earlier rainstorms wet and seal the clay soils in preparation for something bigger and more mysterious. The White Nile and its eastern tributaries, the Sobat, Pibor and Baro, begin to swell independently of the rains, building steadily into a surge of water. Soon the channels of the Sudd spill over, pushing a broad front of water across the plains, heading ever northwestwards. The area of the swamp under water doubles in size, and vast areas of sun-baked soil are transformed into mirror-like flood plains. The huge herds of white-eared kob and tiang seek refuge together on higher ground in the south.

During the peak of the flood, from June to October, the marshes are left to nature. But they are far from empty. Such a constantly changing water-world presents enormous challenges but, as always, nature has come up with some interesting and often bizarre responses. Strange creatures inhabit the swamps, and this is the season for activity.

A flat-snouted fish, up to 2 m (6.5 feet) long and weighing up to 17 kg (37 lb) emerges from the mud. This is a lungfish, whose 300-million-year-old design enables it to get around the problem of drought and flood by sitting out the dry times deep underground. It waits in suspended animation, wrapped in a protective cocoon of its own mucus, breathing through primitive lungs. A catfish called *Clarias* can also breathe if it has to, but it does not have a time capsule in which to wait for the flood. It walks to it, using its pectoral fins like little elbows, which are able to haul it long distances through the constantly changing mosaic of land and water, and heads out into the newly flooded grasslands to feed and breed.

There are antelopes that are equally well adapted to this semi-aquatic life. Sitatungas have long legs, with specially splayed and elongated hooves and flexible toe joints which together act like snowshoes on soft ground. Among the most aquatic of all antelopes, they can feed whilst submerged to shoulder height and are even reasonable swimmers if necessary. Sitatungas are shy, moving slowly and deliberately through the water plants, lifting each leg clear of the water and then carefully slipping it back in with the hoof angled straight down – a watery tiptoe that ensures they are as quiet as possible. They work their way along a network of tunnels and pathways through the dense swamp, free of competition from other, more land-loving antelopes. If spooked, a sitatunga will flee into deeper water, often submerging itself completely with nothing showing except a nervous pair of nostrils.

Opposite: Like all animals that live in the swamps of southern Sudan, the shy, semi-aquatic Sitatunga antelope has to put up with hordes of biting insects.

Below: Special leg-like fins allow the lungfish to walk across land if it needs to. Protected in a cocoon of mud and mucus through the dry season, it may have to walk some distance to find a pool of water when it emerges in the wet season.

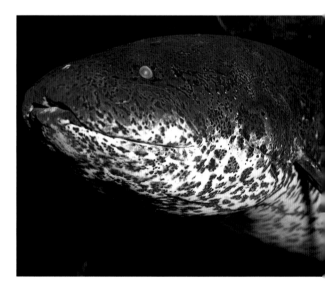

Overleaf: A nomadic life is the best survival strategy for the people of the Sudd's ever-changing mosaic of land and water.

**Left:** Dense stands of papyrus provide perfect cover for the shoebill stork, one of the most bizarre and elusive inhabitants of the Sudd swamps.

**Below:** The art of spear-fishing is a key skill handed down through generations of Dinka society.

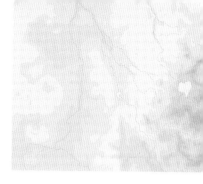

The shallow water of the temporary flood plains is a rich resource for birds as it contains ripe grass seeds, crustaceans, molluscs, aquatic insects and enormous numbers of fish. Storks, herons, egrets, ibis, pelicans, geese, ducks, waders and passerine seed-eaters crowd the plains in their tens of thousands. Some birds use the Sudd as a vital stopover on their north–south migration or as a winter refuge. For others the Sudd is a permanent home. The most notable of the resident birds is the extraordinary shoebill – a huge, blue-grey stork that stands over 1 m (3 feet) tall.

By November the influx of water via river surge and rain is over and, as the flood waters begin to recede, many Dinka and Nuer become fishermen, some spearing fish in shallow water, others using dugout canoes and nets. But they have to be careful. Huge Nile crocodiles are also out fishing. It is not unusual for fishermen to bear scars, or even lose limbs, from the tense relationship between the Sudd's top fish-hunters. A gentler hunter, and one that is no threat to the fishermen, is the spotted-necked otter. Its long tail, well-webbed and clawed toes, and

Below: The Nile monitor lizard is well adapted to the Sudd's changing habitats. Equally happy on land and in water, it can hunt for its own food or will scavenge from others.

keen eyes are ideal for chasing small fish through the underwater labyrinth of leaves, stems and roots at the margins of the main channels. Its larger cousin, the clawless otter, chooses to hunt crabs and frogs amongst the dense swamp vegetation.

The most adaptable of all the Sudd's hunters is the Nile monitor. A smaller cousin of Asia's infamous Komodo dragon, this lizard can nevertheless grow to 2 m (6.5 feet) long and exhibits the fierce temperament, powerful claws and dangerous bite one would expect from a dragon. Perfectly designed for the ever-changing Sudd, the Nile monitor is happy on land, but in its element under water where it is fast and nimble in pursuit of fish.

With the end of the rains the strong tropical sun continues to beat down on the shallow wet-season marshes and the water begins to evaporate. The Sudd's next big change is under way. Day by day, as the White Nile's food-rich waters shrink towards the permanent marshes and channels, a new gift of the river is revealed – a lush carpet of flood-plain grass, refreshed and fertilized by months under water. This is the prelude to the Sudd's most spectacular wildlife event, and the answer to the question posed earlier of how the Sudd could support such huge numbers of animals and people.

Wave after wave of tiang, kob and gazelles follow the huge green carpet as it rolls out – the start of a mass migration. Although they shared flood-season refuges on higher ground, the tiang and kob now part company. The tiang and the gazelles head steadily northwest, 400 km (250 miles) to the Nile flood plain in the centre of the Sudd. The kob strike off northeast, walking 1500 km (930 miles) to the plains of the Pibor river.

The Dinka and Nuer, of course, respond to the same natural rhythm with their own migration. They walk their cattle ever further from their villages as the flood waters recede, a steady movement that will bring them to the river banks by the peak of the dry season. This is the high point of their year. With their precious cattle thriving on the wide green pastures and fish still plentiful, living is comparatively easy.

With everything on the move, it is not long before the paths of the tiang, gazelles and kob cross those of people and their cattle. It is a natural opportunity for the tribesmen to hunt. Tiang and gazelles are the most common quarry, though some tribes hunt kob. As the Dinka and Nuer eat the meat of their cattle only rarely, this wild harvest can account for up to a quarter of the meat in their diet. Most antelopes are dispatched with spears after they have been run down with dogs. But the civil war and the inevitable spread of the automatic weapon has created a bleak

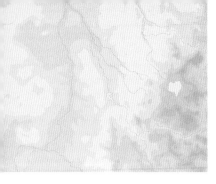

prospect for the great migrating herds. As the Sudd remains a barrier to scientists, it is still not known how the tiang, gazelles and kob are surviving this chapter in its history. It is to be hoped they will not go the way of the swamp's elephants. Once a huge population that ranged over the whole region, the elephants fell prey to ivory hunters in the nineteenth and twentieth centuries. Today's relatively small herds have become swamp animals, hiding in dense papyrus for much of the year and only venturing out at the peak of the flood when the waters afford some protection.

While the Sudd's flood is impressive, it is not the one that helped to nourish ancient Egypt. During the wet season, the swamp soaks up water like a sponge and spreads it in a thin film over a huge area. Rather than surging on downstream, much of the water simply evaporates. In fact, the tropical sun burns away not only all the influx from rain but also nearly half the river-surge water: the White Nile leaves the Sudd with only half the power with which it entered. Instead, the answer to the Nile's flood is found up the smaller, narrower Blue Nile.

## THE BLUE NILE

For more than 500 km (310 miles) upstream from Khartoum the Blue Nile winds its way through flat, semi-desert scrub and savannah. Beyond the border with Ethiopia things begin to change. Out of the dry-season haze rises a mountain range which, closer to, looks like a solid wall of rock. The course of the river up to this point was almost certainly known to the Kushites, and maybe even the ancient Egyptians had heard of it. But from here onwards it was a different matter. The Blue Nile disappears into the belly of the mountains, via an increasingly impassable gorge with fearsome rapids.

Superstition has long held that the gorge is an evil place populated by dangerous spirits, and it has always been a serious obstacle in the search for the river's source. The tenacious Turko–Egyptian invaders and Victorian explorers of the nineteenth century were defeated by it, and it continued to claim many lives in the twentieth century. It was only in 1968 that the gorge was finally navigated. Even today, rumours of terrible rapids, huge crocodiles and ruthless bandits deter would-be travellers.

Heading up the gorge, it soon becomes apparent that its hot dry bottom and its cool green rim, over 1000 m (3300 feet) above, are a world apart. In fact, the bottom of the gorge merely represents an extension of Sudan's savannah into Ethiopia's mountain world. The only oases in this

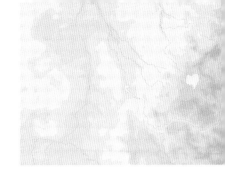

semi-desert occur where small rivers flowing across the mountain plateau above hurl themselves off the gorge's cliffs to join the Blue Nile below. Their spray allows tiny patches of rainforest to cling to the rocks year-round. Paradise flycatchers, parrots, lovebirds, bee-eaters, hoopoes and weaver birds provide tiny splashes of colour and sound as they cash in on locally abundant insects and seeds. Slender-billed, chestnut-winged starlings go a step further and use the mini-waterfalls as protective barriers, flying through the curtains of water to roost and breed on small rock ledges.

In the dry season the Blue Nile gorge is a semi-desert, but there are clues that it is not always so. The rocks by the waterfalls indicate that there are times when the flow of water is much stronger. The water-worn rocks of the main river show that it increases in width. Dead vegetation caught in surrounding trees could only have been put there by a powerful water force.

## THE ETHIOPIAN HIGHLANDS

After 600 km (370 miles) of dry gorge the landscape of the Blue Nile changes again. The river flows across a mountain plateau in the centre of the Ethiopian Highlands. At an altitude of 1800 m (5900 feet), this cooler mountain world sets Ethiopia apart from the rest of Africa – an amazing 80 per cent of the continent's mountains are found here. Wide plateaus are fringed by yet higher ground, where trees cannot grow and moorland takes over.

This land has a violent geological past. It sits on the edge of Africa's Great Rift Valley, a huge wrinkle in the earth's surface that thrust Ethiopia's mountains skywards between 40 million and 25 million years ago. Over time, layer upon layer of black volcanic basalt poured out through weaknesses in the earth's fabric, setting hard to form the Ethiopian mountain plateau. As the basalt cooled, and after major tectonic shifts, cracks developed in the dome. During the ice ages that followed, high precipitation and the usual battering by winds resulted in the rapid erosion of the cracks – and a spectacular landscape. On one side the land sweeps gently across a highland bowl, punctuated only by the Blue Nile's gorge. On the other side, the mountains drop precipitously thousands of metres to a desert world far below. Along this imposing edge, towers of rock and near-vertical cliffs stretch as far as the eye can see. It is among the most beautiful sights in Africa.

The Ethiopian Highlands are one of the continent's harshest environments. But they are far from devoid of life. It is more than wind that makes the dry vegetation twitch and quiver. Little brown furry heads poke up from low vantage points, ears scan like radar dishes, while beady eyes

Previous page: A host of small streams and rivers forms a huge network of waterways across the Ethiopian Highlands. They all eventually find their way into the enormous gorge of the Blue Nile.

Opposite: The erosion of volcanic rock over millions of years has has created some of Africa's most striking mountain scenery: the Ethiopian Highlands.

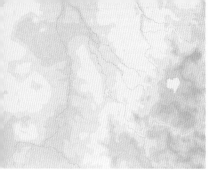

stare nervously out from a tiny world of dry, grassy tunnels and trails. The apparently dead, dry tangle of vegetation is, in fact, alive with rodents.

Amazingly, these African moorlands support one of the world's highest densities of these animals. There may be up to 3 tonnes of rodents per square kilometre (less than half a square mile) in a good year, each species choosing a slightly different diet from a menu of leaves, roots, seeds and insects. They overcome lack of shelter by living in tunnels, either partially or completely under ground. But the mountain weather is not all they need to shelter from. With this number of rodents, there are, of course, predators.

The hills are home to Ethiopian wolves, a species unique to this region. Much smaller than true wolves, these handsome, long-legged mouse-hunters are sometimes, more appropriately, called Simien jackals. Watching them hunt is an education in patience and stealth. They work alone, using a stalk-and-pounce approach as their preferred technique. A wolf will lie motionless for long periods, its attractive, rich russet-red coat blending with the parched vegetation. All the while eyes, nose and particularly ears are trained on the tangle of grass ahead, waiting for a rodent to arrive at the mouth of a tunnel. The wolf waits: the body tenses and then explodes, springing high in the air before landing with all four feet together, pinning the ill-fated rodent to the ground. A long snout grabs the meal. A quick shake of the wolf's head and its prey is dead.

Left: The rich volcanic soils of the Ethiopian Highlands support one of the highest densities of rodents in the world.

Opposite: The Ethiopian wolf is an expert rat-catcher. A long, thin snout armed with sharp teeth is ideal for snatching rodents from their holes.

Overleaf: The giant lobelia is one of the few plants that grows tall in the windswept highlands of the Blue Nile, reaching up to 3 m (10 feet) in height.

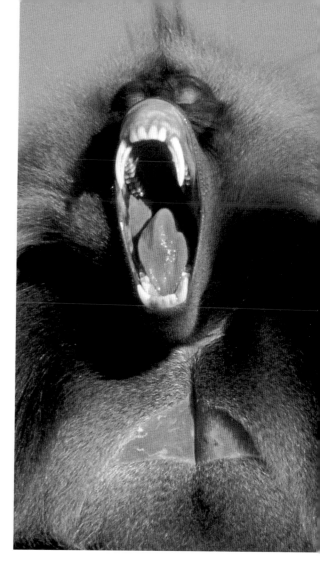

Sadly, the mountain world of the Blue Nile's catchment area is not impervious to change and the handsome Ethiopian wolf may soon be gone for ever. The danger comes from below. The increase in the human population at lower altitudes means that people are encroaching on the wolf's mountain refuge. With people come dogs, which are so closely related to the wolf that interbreeding is diluting its genes in a slow but inexorable biological genocide. A further pressure is global warming, which is shrinking the Ethiopian wolf's mountain habitat. The remaining animals are trapped on ever-smaller islands of highland cool in a rising sea of unnaturally warm air.

Dawn along the precipitous edge finds another emblem of the Ethiopian Highlands emerging, in noisy congregations of up to 600 individuals. Gelada baboons are among the most specialized and striking of all monkeys. The larger males, weighing up to 20 kg (44 lb), look truly formidable. A magnificent lion-like mane frames a long snout bearing fearsome teeth – weapons the males are not averse to displaying with slow and deliberate yawns or by curling back their bright pink lips. At first sight it seems that the local rodents would have much to fear from the geladas – but looks, in this case, are deceiving. Uniquely amongst primates, these spectacular beasts are actually strict grass-eaters. The display of magnificent teeth is mostly symbolic – a display that sorts out who is boss in a highly social society.

From December to April these mountains of the Nile do not seem to offer the lush vegetation needed to support the hordes of rodents or large herbivores such as the geladas. Indeed, drought brings near famine to the geladas, who are forced to pound the dry ground, digging for a survival diet of roots. But their furious digging unearths a darker soil. Here, high on the roof of Africa, thousands of kilometres from the Nile valley of ancient Egypt, is the dark soil of the river's distant flood plains.

## A GIFT FROM THE MOUNTAINS

During the wet season from May to September approximately 2 m (6.5 feet) of rain falls on the Ethiopian Highlands in just a few weeks as a tropical monsoon sweeps in from the Indian Ocean. When it meets the steep slopes of the mountains, it unleashes a freezing deluge of rain and hail. In between storms, intense tropical sunshine pierces the thin mountain air and empowers the refreshed vegetation. The dark soil is rich in nutrients – a legacy of the highlands' volcanic past, when a potent cocktail of minerals welled up from deep inside the earth. This now fuels the rapid growth of a carpet of lush grass and myriad hardy mountain flowers – gelada paradise.

**Above:** The gelada baboon's aggressive appearance belies a more gentle nature. The impressive teeth of this male are used only to display to other males

**Opposite:** Gelada baboons live in complex social groupings in troupes that may number many hundreds.

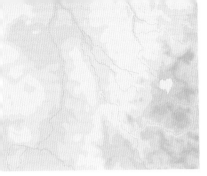

In their labyrinth of tunnels rodents are breeding furiously, cashing in on this ephemeral bounty. Their wet-season menu of flowers reads like a suburban British garden. *Helichrysum*, *Alchemilla* and *Bidens*, plus heather, thyme and cranesbill, all find a home and provide the rodents with an annual feast of flowers. But the animals' activity attracts attention. Augur buzzards, strikingly patterned in black, white and rich chestnut brown, use the huge, telephone-pole-like flower spikes of giant lobelias as sentry posts. Their powerful eyes spot tell-tale quivers in the flower garden below, and their sharp talons follow through.

All over the moorland, the sounds of wind, birds and insects are punctuated by the liquid song of bubbling water. At first the moorland soaks up the rain like a huge sponge, but soon the deluge is so relentless that the land is saturated and the water flows sheet-like across its surface, or bleeds out of the ground in thousands of tiny springs. The rich, dark soil, loosened

**Below:** The dark, nutrient-rich soil of the Ethiopian Highlands is the same soil that fertilized the land of ancient Egypt.

by the nightly freeze and daily thaw of underground ice and the furious burrowing of millions of rodents, is eroded by the quickening pace of the Blue Nile's headwaters. The river's great gift has finally begun its epic journey to Egypt.

These days the magic soil is loosened not only by frosts and rodents but also by human activity. The Ethiopian Highlands are full of people, most of whom subsist by ploughing the soil and sowing seed. Just below moorland level, a gently undulating patchwork of green and brown fields sweeps across the high plateau as far as the eye can see. The farmers grow a mixture of hardy cereals and pulses in what is thought to be the largest contiguous area of cultivated land in Africa.

These scenes of plenty fly in the face of the stereotyped dust-bowl and famine image of Ethiopia. But the rains sometimes fail and famine has been a threat for thousands of years. Admittedly, these wetter highlands are affected last and least when the rains are poor. Food shortages, however, are not necessarily due to poor productivity. They also arise from a lack of storage facilities, which prevents good season excesses from being used in lean years: in addition, the presence of grain pests – in particular weevils – makes long-term storage difficult. Ethiopia's highland people are therefore exposed to the vagaries of the Blue Nile's rains each year.

Every year, towards the end of the rains, the highlanders celebrate Meskal – a sort of harvest festival or thanksgiving for nature's gifts and, in particular, for good rains. The hills around are

Above: During the Meskal festival at the end of the rains, the Ethiopian Highlands are carpeted with *Bidens* flowers, known as Meskal daisies.

carpeted with *Bidens* flowers, giving the plant its local name: 'Meskal daisy'. During the festival one small stream is much celebrated. Flowing down from Mount Gishe, it is thought to be the start of the longest of the Blue Nile's tributaries and is therefore declared to be the source of the Abay, the local name for the river. A series of rituals and ceremonies are performed on the banks of the stream which, although small, personifies the Nile itself in the minds of the Ethiopians.

**Above:** In the flood season a journey by horse may involve a perilous river-crossing. Each year, many Ethiopians are killed by the floodwaters of the Nile.

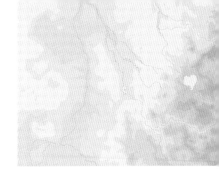

Although the highlanders are predominantly Coptic Christian, a much older, animalistic belief still survives. Some people follow a curious mixture of both, somehow unwilling to sever ties with an ancient belief that connects them to nature. In a place where human beings are so dependent on good soil and water, and fearful of flooding, it is easy to see why. It is therefore not uncommon to find small groups of people huddled by a river bank, quietly chanting verses and throwing offerings into the water – a piece of bread, a cup of coffee or a glass of local firewater. They are making contact with Gihon, the Blue Nile's own river spirit, named after one of the four rivers that were said to have flowed out of Eden at the beginning of the world. Later, a chicken or a sheep may be sacrificed and its blood poured into the muddy water. Devotees ask Gihon for help, or beg for mercy during the floods. Later, they will thank Gihon for a good harvest or for sparing them from flood or famine. These rituals are more low-key than those at the Blue Nile's source, but the quiet conviction with which they are performed suggests that their roots run deeper into history, back to a time when mankind lived even closer to nature.

## THE BLUE NILE SOURCE

In contrast to the source of the White Nile, the Blue Nile source has been known for many hundreds of years. Although too far away to be familiar to the ancient Egyptians, the Ethiopian Highlands have been heavily populated since before the rise of the Christian kingdom of Axum in the fourth century AD. The Blue Nile system, with its massive gorge, dominates both the landscape and the lives of the highland people who inhabit the area. Its course is clear and the position of its source has long been established as a landmark in the world of the highlanders.

The source of the Blue Nile at Mount Gishe first appeared on European maps more than 150 years before the famous Victorian explorers of the mid-nineteenth century even started to look for the source of the White Nile. The first Europeans to describe the Blue Nile source were Pedro Paez and Jerome Lobo, both Portuguese Jesuit priests. Paez and Lobo had entered what was then Abyssinia from the Indian Ocean in 1611 and reached the source in April 1618. But this event was not widely reported in Europe. The glory for the 'discovery' of the Blue Nile's source was, in fact, claimed in the late eighteenth century by James Bruce, a larger-than-life Scottish explorer who was a precursor of the Victorian explorers. His jealous hatred of the Jesuit priests who had come to the region before him drove Bruce to discount their previous descriptions. He replaced them with assertions of his own, including the claim that the Blue Nile was the main stream and the White Nile a mere tributary. Bruce was determined to go down in history as having discovered the source of the Nile. During a ten-year expedition to the region,

he reached Mount Gishe on 4 November 1770 and claimed the discovery for himself. But his ego was to be his undoing. Returning to London in 1774, his exaggerated assertions were rejected by the academic community, and the book he published in 1790 was ridiculed as 'romantic fiction'. Four years later, Bruce died without the glory he craved. Since then, the more modest accounts of Paez and Lobo have been accepted as the first European descriptions of the source of the Blue Nile.

## THE START OF THE FLOOD

The Blue Nile's innumerable tributaries eventually flow to the bottom of Ethiopia's high mountain bowl, where the land is almost flat. As the churning brown water fans out through a dense stand of papyrus, it seems that the gathering force of the river has been diffused. A rich and complex noise rises from the marsh – a weaver bird colony. Papyrus provides a perfect home for weavers, safe in their bustling city of nests above the swampy water, and its flowers are a useful building material.

**Above:** Although expert fish-catchers themselves, pelicans also follow Lake Tana's fishermen for a free meal of fish scraps.

**Opposite above:** The making of papyrus canoes, or *tankwas*, is a long-held Nilotic tradition still practised on Lake Tana.

**Opposite below:** His nest of woven papyrus complete, a male weaver bird displays to watching females.

**Overleaf:** Tis Isat Falls in Ethiopia is an excellent place to witness the enormous power of the Blue Nile's great flood.

The bright yellow and black males weave long threads of the reeds into the most tempting nests they can muster, then launch into a flamboyant display to prospective mates, hanging upside down from their show homes, wings outstretched like flags of invitation. People are also collecting papyrus for weaving, but they take whole stems to make extremely buoyant canoes – *tankwas*. This papyrus technology is used all along the Nile and has changed little from that of ancient Egypt.

But this is not a Sudd-like swamp. It is the papyrus fringe of a huge lake – Lake Tana, the Blue Nile's own inland sea, so wide that you cannot see across it and covering more than 3000 sq km (1160 square miles). Although relatively shallow, it represents a significant reservoir for the Blue Nile's precious water. It is thought that the ancient Egyptians had heard about this huge mountain lake, even if they did not recognize its significance in their own lives. Lake Tana has always supported a healthy fishing industry and every evening its waters are dotted with men in *tankwas* setting nets. The next morning boats laden with fish head for shore, many followed by an expectant queue of hungry pelicans.

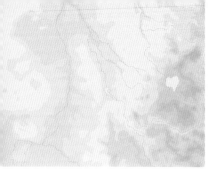

At the end of the wet season Lake Tana may be nearly 2 m (6.5 feet) higher than its dry-season level, so an impressive head of water is built up. Although around 60 rivers flow into the lake, only one flows out. This is the Blue Nile – the Abay Wenz (great river). But, for such a great river, the Blue Nile has a relatively inauspicious start. What many consider to be its true source is nothing more than a bend in the lake's shoreline, where a calm-looking river, less than 100 m (330 feet) wide, slips quietly behind a screen of boulders and reeds.

Below: The spectacular Blue Nile gorge is Africa's Grand Canyon.

What the Blue Nile lacks in its initial departure, it soon makes up for just a few kilometres downstream. Flowing strongly yet calmly, with hardly a rapid to ruffle its surface, the great river suddenly plunges off a sheer rocky step more than 45 m (150 feet) high. In one giant leap, a sedate river is transformed into a boiling cauldron. This waterfall, the second biggest in Africa, is called Tis Isat, meaning 'smoking fire' – a reference to the huge columns of spray that can be seen from miles around. Virtually dry in June, by September it has swollen tenfold into a wall of water and mud over 400 m (1310 feet) across. This is a force powerful enough to carry an amazing 140 million tonnes of mud and silt thousands of kilometres to Egypt every year.

Tis Isat marks the start of the mighty Blue Nile gorge. Over a million years, the river's flood carved this huge gash through the highlands of Ethiopia. Well over 1000 m (3300 feet) deep in places, and nearly 20 km (12 miles) wide, it is Africa's Grand Canyon. More huge rivers – the Beshilo, Jema, Muger, Guder and Didissa – join the Blue Nile, adding their own massive loads of water and silt to a raging torrent that triples in size along the gorge's twisting arc, some 600 km (370 miles) long. Emerging from its steep rocky water chute, the great flood races on across the savannah plains of Sudan to meet the White Nile at Khartoum, a confluence that is now 400 times larger than it was in the dry season.

At the peak of the flood the Blue Nile is far more powerful than the steady White Nile. In fact, 60 per cent of the flood waters that reach Egypt come from the Blue Nile. The White Nile, by contrast, contributes a mere 14 per cent and the rest of the water comes from two large tributaries, the Sobat and the Atbara. Such is the power of the Blue Nile in flood that it pens the White Nile's waters in a huge lake upstream of Khartoum.

The Blue Nile provides the answer to the riddle of the Nile's great flood and the Nile valley's fertility. But out of the short flood season it dwindles and contributes little to the river's flow. It was the steady flow of the White Nile, regardless of season, that was the ancient Egyptians' lifeline between the yearly floods. So where do the White Nile's waters come from that gives them such stability? The Sudd's flood adds little to the system downstream, so the reason for the river's reliable flow must lie yet further upstream. The White Nile stretches back into the heart of Africa, to the mountains of Uganda and beyond. It is even longer than the Blue Nile, so it harbours the Nile's furthest tributary and, by definition, the great river's true source. It is the White Nile's headwaters that hold the secret of the Nile's steady flow through Egypt between floods. But, as is so often the case with this river, it did not reveal its secret easily. The search for the source of the White Nile is an age-old quest that has taxed many, but came to obsess the explorers of the Victorian era.

CHAPTER 3

# THE SEARCH
## FOR THE
# SOURCE

The nature and origin of the Nile's source mystified mankind for centuries. As long ago as 460 BC the Greek historian Herodotus journeyed up the Nile looking for its source, but reached only the first cataract at Aswan before turning back. The Emperor Nero sent an expedition south in the first century AD, but its way was blocked by an impassable swamp and it, too, turned back with no answers. Successive expeditions up the river, even as late as the early nineteenth century, fared little better. They were defeated by the vast swamp of the Sudd, by debilitating diseases, an unforgiving climate, and by the hostility of local tribes. So while America and Australia were explored, the Nile's source remained a mystery.

The first-known map of the river was drawn by the Greek geographer and astronomer Ptolemy in the middle of the second century BC. His map was based on the legend of a Greek merchant, Diogenes, who had 'travelled inland for 25-days' journey and arrived in the vicinity of two great lakes, and the snowy range of mountains whence the Nile draws its twin sources'.

Above: Stanley Glacier, high in the Ruwenzori range. For centuries there were rumours that the Nile issued from snow-capped mountains in the heart of Africa. These rumours were generally dismissed as fanciful tales.

Ptolemy's map with its 'Mountains of the Moon' remained unchanged until the middle of the nineteenth century.

Arab traders had long been plying their wares along the east and north coasts of Africa, exchanging manufactured goods for gold, ivory and slaves, and they had heard rumours of great lakes and mountains. But it was not until the sultan of Oman moved his court to Zanzibar in 1832 that the trading routes into the interior of Africa really opened up. The Arabs discovered a number of great lakes inland, but news of these reached Europe only in the middle of the century when two German missionaries in east Africa, Johann Rebmann and Jacob Erhardt, produced a map based on the Arab traders' reports. It showed a large, slug-like lake – the sea of Ujiji or the sea of Tanganyika – in the middle of Africa.

Speculation that this great lake might be the source of the Nile was the catalyst for Britain's Royal Geographical Society to launch an expedition into the interior of central Africa. Victorian Britain was ripe for such a quest. There was an economic interest in opening up trade routes and establishing a new sphere of influence. There was a moral motive: abolition of the slave trade was a popular Victorian cause, and where better to start than at its root? And there was the probability of new discoveries of flora and fauna: the Victorians were always on the lookout for new specimens for their museums. Add to this the healthy romanticism of geographical exploration, and an expedition to the source of the Nile was inevitable. And the person most suited to lead the expedition was not hard to find. His name was Richard Burton.

**Left:** Sir Richard Francis Burton in 1876. An exceptional linguist, a maverick soldier and diplomat, Burton was one of the most charismatic explorers of the Victorian era.

**Opposite:** Captain John Hanning Speke in 1863. Although Speke's discoveries were key to identifying the Nile's sources he died before they were fully accepted by the establishment.

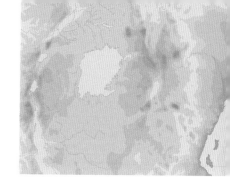

# TO LAKE TANGANYIKA

Richard Burton was born to adventure. From an early age he was bored by middle-class comfort and kicked against authority. He was expelled from Oxford for 'disorderly behaviour' and received a string of reprimands when he served in the Indian Army. But he was an intellectual giant and had a prodigious ability to learn languages. It was a combination of his interest in anthropology and geography, and his linguistic skills, that made him an accomplished explorer. He might, indeed, have been recognized as the greatest of all Victorian explorers had it not been for his insatiable fascination with everything around him. Burton often preferred to record some new detail of tribal dress or custom than race up the next hill to see what lay beyond. This, in the end, was his undoing.

Burton chose John Hanning Speke as his companion. The two men had ventured into Somalia together in 1854 and neither had fared well, nor did they particularly like each other, so it was a strange choice. Ostensibly, Speke had little to offer. His prime interest was in shooting game; he came with no scientific credentials; he spoke no languages; and, unlike Burton, he was apparently uninterested in literature and learning. He was, however, methodical, courageous and had a determination that even Burton admired. He was also exceedingly ambitious. Burton was setting off not with a devoted student but with a rival for the glory given to successful explorers.

Burton's expedition was to approach the great lake – or lakes – of central Africa via the trading routes from the east coast. Accordingly, he and Speke sailed for the island of Zanzibar in 1856. During the rainy season they explored the coast of the mainland, searching out the best route inland, and in June 1857 landed their stores at Bagamoyo in modern-day Tanzania. It turned out to be an inauspicious beginning. On arrival their chief guide, whom they had sent ahead, reported that he had managed to contract only 36 porters. They needed upward of 170 to carry all their equipment. Reluctantly, they resorted to donkeys.

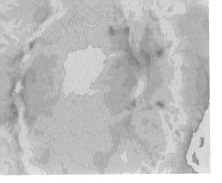

They had provisions for nearly two years. Their personal baggage included tents, beds, mosquito netting, blankets, chairs, a table, a small library, journals, fishing rods and carpenters' tools – all the necessities for gentlemen travelling rough. They also had to take the scientific books and instruments necessary for their geographic research. Since their plan was to buy staple foods along the way, the only foodstuffs they carried were essentials such as salt, sugar and tea. But they also had to take cooking pots and utensils. And trade goods that would pay for food and appease tribal chiefs en route – beads, brass wire and yard upon yard of cloth – were vital.

The need for large quantities of trade goods was due, in part, to their choice of route. They had resolved to take a well-worn Arab slave route into the interior rather than blaze their own trail. But the chieftains who lived along the way had become greedy for tribute from passing foreigners and were inclined to tax slavers, traders and explorers alike.

As the expedition set off inland, problems soon arose. The donkeys reared, bucked and threw their loads, making progress chaotic. The motley crew of guards, guides and porters, accompanied by their wives, children and cattle, began to argue amongst themselves and desertions followed. Speke fell ill with fever and Burton was weary: 'The new life, the alternations of damp heat and wet cold, the useless fatigue of walking, the sorry labour of waiting and reloading the asses, the exposure to sun and dew, and last, but not least, of morbific influences, the wear and tear of mind at the prospect of imminent failure, all were beginning to tell heavily on me.' They had been on the road less than a week.

Left: Sidi Bombay. Engaged first by Burton as a gun-bearer, with the responsibilities of an officer, he proved himself indispensable, and both Speke and later Stanley hired him as a factotum.

Snail-like, they made their way through forest, bog and savannah, across rivers and over an escarpment on to the central plateau of the region. After nearly five months, they reached a town that Burton and Speke called Kazeh, but which was commonly known as Tabora. This was a central hub for Arab traders and slave caravans coming from the south, west and north en route to the coast. Here Burton and Speke rested, dismissed most of their men and sorted out their remaining stores. Burton was at ease, happy to converse with and be amongst Arabs, whose culture he enjoyed, but he soon fell seriously ill again. Speke, hungry for information, continued to question Arabs about the geography of the outlying regions, using Sidi Bombay, their trusty 'man Friday', as an interpreter. He later described one particular conversation:

*On my opening Messrs Rebmann and Erhardt's map, and asking him where Nyasa was, he said it was a distinct lake from Ujiji, lying to the southward. This opened our eyes to a most interesting fact, for the first time discovered. I then asked what the word Ukéréwé meant, and was answered in the same way, that it was a lake to the northward, much larger than Ujiji, and this solved the mystery. The missionaries had run three lakes into one.*

Speke learnt that the three lakes were: Nyasa (Lake Malawi) to the south, Ujiji (Lake Tanganyika) to the west and the 'Sea of Ukéréwé' (Lake Victoria) to the north. At this point he felt strongly that the sea of Ukéréwé was the lake they should be investigating, but Burton insisted on keeping to their original plan: to explore the lake at Ujiji. The two men were openly at odds.

They set off westwards with a complement of fresh porters, but as Burton had to be carried, their pace remained pitifully slow. In January 1858 Burton suffered such a bad attack of malaria that he thought he was going to die. His legs became palsied and for the rest of the year he was unable to walk any distance at all. Speke was not much better off. He was still suffering from bouts of fever and these were compounded by anaemia, trachoma and ophthalmia. He suffered 'an almost total blindness, rendering every object enclouded as by a misty veil'.

The two bone-weary, desperately sick men persevered doggedly, while their porters, believing their employers would die, continued to steal from them at will. On 13 February they were

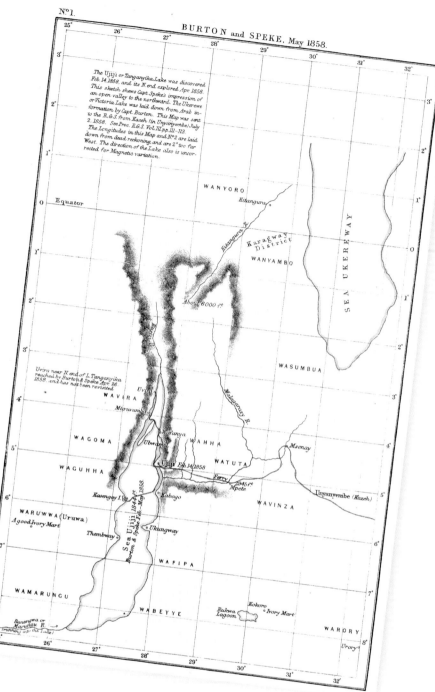

**Above:** Map of Burton and Speke's route from Kazeh (now Tabora) to Lake Tanganyika, or Lake Ujiji. The northern lake, here called Ukereway, was renamed Lake Victoria by Speke.

making their way up an unforgiving rocky hill when Speke's donkey collapsed underneath him and died. But at the top of the hill Burton saw a glimmering light beneath him. The explorers had, at last, reached their goal. Burton was euphoric:

*Nothing, in sooth, could be more picturesque than this first view of the Tanganyika Lake, as it lay in the lap of the mountains, basking in the gorgeous tropical sunshine ... truly it was a revel for soul and sight! Forgetting toils, dangers, and the doubtfulness of return, I felt willing to endure double what I had endured; and all the party seemed to join with me in joy. My purblind companion found nothing to grumble at except the 'mist and glare before his eyes'.*

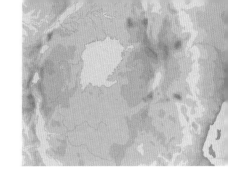

Speke, standing close by, felt rather differently:

*Here you may picture to yourself my bitter disappointment when, after toiling through so many miles of savage life, all the time emaciated by divers sicknesses and weakened by great privations of food and rest, I found, on approaching the zenith of my ambition, the Great Lake in question nothing but mist and glare before my eyes. From the summit of the eastern horn the lovely Tanganyika Lake could be seen in all its glory by everybody but myself.*

The town of Ujiji was a massive disappointment to Burton as it was only a smattering of huts on the shore of the lake, certainly not the hub that Tabora had been. Moreover, Speke was getting on his nerves. Still an invalid, Burton decided to send his companion off to explore the northern reaches of the lake, but Speke returned within the month having failed in his mission. His only new intelligence was that there was rumoured to be a river at the northern end of the lake. While he had been away Burton himself had heard that this same river, the Ruzizi, flowed out of the lake.

Speke's news steeled Burton into rising from his sickbed and procuring two open canoes. This time the explorers set out together to investigate the river but their men, who were not used to rowing, were less than enthusiastic. As they proceeded up the narrow lake, local people they encountered told of ferocious tribes to the north. Finally, the crew mutinied and even the loyal Bombay refused to go further. Burton could not persuade even one man to take him the remaining 32 km (20 miles) to the end of the lake, so fearsome was the reputation of the tribes there. But information – even if it was not what Burton wanted to hear – could be gleaned from three local people they met at this point. 'They … unanimously asserted, and every man in the host of bystanders confirmed their words, that the "Rusisi" enters into, and does not flow out of the Tanganyika. I felt sick at heart.' It was a bitter blow to Burton, who must have realized that the riddle of the Nile's source would not be easily solved.

The expedition returned to Ujiji where Burton decided that they did not have the resources to explore the southern end of the lake. They began to prepare for the long march home and, on 28 May 1858, left Ujiji to return to Tabora. On arrival there it was clear that both explorers needed to rest. Burton's hands and feet were swollen and Speke could hardly see. He was also deaf, the result of an unfortunate incident with a beetle that had bored its way into his eardrum leaving him in considerable pain. But while Burton was happy to recuperate slowly, Speke was champing at the bit, keen to investigate the lake to the north that they had heard about when they first arrived in Tabora. It was now that Burton made the greatest mistake of his life: he sent Speke north with instructions to return within three months.

Glad to be rid of his irritating, complaining companion, and with time to regain his health and organize the return march to the coast, Burton was content. He had his meticulous notes on the geography, botany, geology and meteorology of their journey to write up. In his mind they had achieved their goal by reaching Lake Tanganyika and he felt the expedition had been a success. Little did he realize that Speke, enormously ambitious and with an insatiable appetite to explore and to be first, would make the most significant discovery yet that was relevant to the source of the Nile. Burton had missed his chance.

Speke left Tabora and headed northwards with 30 men. After only 25 days of hard walking they mounted a hill and saw an immense lake. Speke wrote: 'The vast expanse of the pale-blue water of the N'yanza [lake] burst suddenly upon my gaze … I no longer felt any doubt that the lake at my feet gave birth to that interesting river, the source of which has been the subject of so much speculation, and the object of so many explorers.' He named the lake Victoria Nyanza (Lake Victoria) 'after our gracious sovereign'. After only three days on its southern shores, he concluded that it was the source of the Nile.

When Speke told Burton about his great discovery on his return to Tabora, Burton was characteristically scathing about his endeavours: 'We had scarcely breakfasted, before he announced to me the startling fact that he had discovered the sources of the White Nile. It was an inspiration perhaps … The fortunate discoverer's conviction was strong; his reasons were weak …' Burton knew Speke was basing his theory on faith and hearsay and that there was not a shred of supporting evidence. Speke thought Burton was jealous of his prize, and the gap between the two men widened yet further. They did not have enough provisions to make further forays to this new lake, and there was nothing for it but to head home. The atmosphere during their return to the coast was frosty and, by mutual consent, the Nile was not mentioned. The journey took another four gruelling months, during which Speke nearly died from pleurisy and pneumonia.

Both men harboured hopes of a return expedition to Lake Victoria but Speke's ambition may, at this point, have got the better of him. According to Burton, who broke his journey home to convalesce in Aden, Speke's parting words to him were: 'Goodbye, old fellow; you may be quite sure I shall not go up to the Royal Geographical Society until you come to the fore and we appear together. Make your mind easy about that.' Yet the first thing Speke did when he arrived in England was reveal his findings and his theory that Lake Victoria was the source of the Nile to the Society. Thus it was he, and not Burton, who was fêted as a hero and asked to return to Africa. The two men never spoke to each other again.

# LAKE VICTORIA REVISITED

Speke expounded his theory to Sir Roderick Murchison, president of the Royal Geographical Society, and, after speaking to members of the society, he was invited to lead the follow-up expedition. His instructions were to circumnavigate Lake Victoria, find the source of the Nile and follow the river downstream to Gondokoro, south of the Sudd. From there he would continue to Egypt. He was to be at Gondokoro in December 1861, where the British vice-consul, John Petherick, would have a boat and supplies for his onward journey.

Speke asked an army friend, James Augustus Grant, to join the expedition. Where Burton had chosen a rival, Speke preferred someone he could be sure would not challenge his leadership or steal his fame. Grant was an accomplished soldier, but he was also dutiful, loyal, quiet and ultimately self-effacing. Moreover, he was devoted to Speke.

After a long trip round the Cape of Good Hope the two men started their journey into the interior of Africa on 25 September 1860. The starting point was Bagamoyo, as Speke and Burton's had been. They followed the same route as the previous expedition, and experienced the same troubles and frustrations: they had to bribe their way from chieftain to chieftain, their men deserted them, and their animals and goods were stolen. In Tabora they were obliged to wait for seven weeks because of rains and flooding that barred the route north and made it difficult to hire porters.

By then it was early in 1861, and time lost was a worry because of the planned rendezvous with Petherick in December of that year. However, they were able to use these weeks to gather information from the Arabs about the best route around Lake Victoria. It seemed that three powerful kingdoms dominated the north and west sides of the lake: Bunyoro to the north,

Above: Captain James Augustus Grant in 1863. Modest and not overtly ambitious, Grant was the perfect companion for Speke.

Buganda sandwiched in the middle and Karagwe, the southernmost kingdom, to the west. They were governed by kings of very different character, and the intelligence Speke gathered in Tabora proved to be invaluable.

It was 15 November 1861, over a year after leaving the coast, before they reached Karagwe, the first of the kingdoms. There, much to their relief, they were welcomed by Rumanika, a kind, generous and interested king. Unusually, it was the explorers who received gifts on entering the kingdom, rather than the king who demanded them. Rumanika was content with a red blanket.

An interesting aspect of Rumanika's court was that his wives, and the wives of the princes, were enormously fat. They had a steady flow of milk from gourds hanging from the ceiling, and had been fed in this way from childhood. Their obesity was such that they could not stand up, and they remained in their huts like captive seals. Speke described one such lady: 'She could not rise; and so large were her arms that, between the joints, the flesh hung down like large, loose-stuffed puddings.'

**Above:** Speke presenting King Rumanika with spoils from a hunting trip. Rumanika's response was: 'Well ... neither the Arabs nor the Nnanaji could have accomplished such a great feat as this. It is no wonder the English are the greatest men in the world.'

Speke and Grant had been at Rumanika's court for six weeks when, in January 1862, they finally received the invitation they needed in order to proceed to the neighbouring kingdom of Buganda. This was governed by the highly unpredictable Mtesa, a king with a murderous reputation to whom Rumanika paid tribute. Grant was suffering from an ulcerated leg and Rumanika warned him that Mtesa would not tolerate sick men. So Grant stayed behind while Speke marched north into the lion's den. En route he crossed the Kagera river and noted that it was a significant feeder for Lake Victoria. He also glimpsed the lake itself and was once more convinced that this immense inland sea was the source of the Nile. (Given that his brief was to circumnavigate the lake, it is strange that he did not even visit its shores, but proceeded around it well inland. On his return to England to claim the glory for achieving his goal, this was one of the weaknesses in his evidence.)

Speke was pleasantly surprised at the sophistication of Mtesa's palace and the fertility of the country. He recognized its great trading potential but, more pressingly, realized that he had to appease its all-powerful king. He wanted to appear 'rather as a prince than a trader, for the

**Below:** King Mtesa holding a levee. His subjects would be brought before him and sentenced to death on the slightest pretext.

**Overleaf:** More like an inland sea, Lake Victoria is the largest lake in Africa.

purpose of better gaining the confidence of the king'. He wore his best clothes and assembled an impressive entourage, each member of which carried a flag, a gun or a gift. The first meeting with Mtesa did not go well. Speke was kept waiting in the sun, grew exasperated and stalked off. He was asked to sit on the ground but refused. Finally, when he and the king were seated together, a privilege unheard of in Mtesa's court, the exchange of gifts took place. Speke presented rifles, a gold watch, a telescope, beads, silks and a full set of cutlery, while Mtesa proffered cattle, goats, fish, porcupines and rats.

It was the guns that really interested Mtesa. He asked Speke to demonstrate their magic by dispatching four cows. Having done so, Speke witnessed the king's true nature at first-hand:

*The king now loaded one of the carbines I had given him with his own hands, and giving it full-cock to a page, told him to go out and shoot a man in the outer court: which was no sooner accomplished than the little urchin returned to announce his success, with a look of glee such as one would see in the face of a boy who had robbed a bird's-nest, caught a trout, or done any other boyish trick … but the affair created hardly any interest. I never heard, and there appeared no curiosity to know, what individual human being the urchin had deprived of life.*

Mtesa mutilated, tortured and murdered his subjects on the slightest pretext. Almost every day someone would be marched off to be beheaded for some breach of conduct, whether it be talking too loudly or not closing a door. Speke's

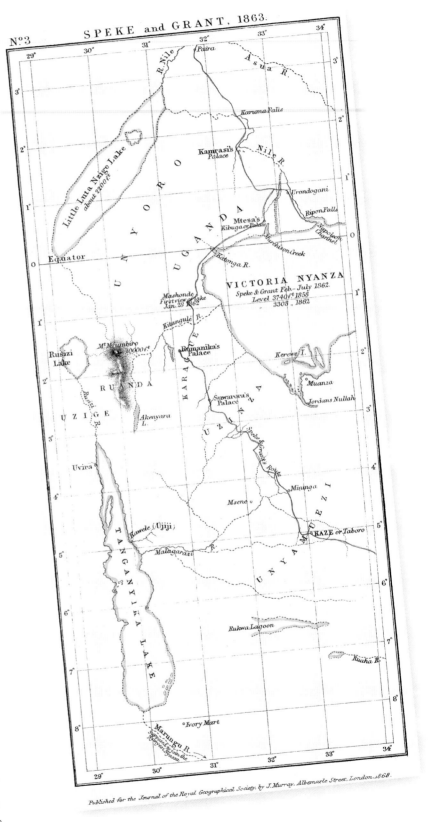

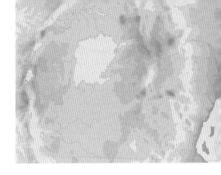

interpreters were so concerned for their lives that they did not dare to speak to Mtesa before he spoke to them. This, of course, slowed the progress of Speke's diplomatic negotiations. As well as wanting to glean information about the terrain that lay ahead, he was keen to request permission for Grant to be admitted to the kingdom.

Grant limped into Mtesa's court three months after Speke's arrival and the two men exchanged their news. They had both heard of a river that flowed north out of Lake Victoria and Speke was itching to get going. He was sure he was about to discover the source of the Nile. They duly sought permission to leave, but Mtesa was still amused by his two white guests and detained them for a further six weeks. Exasperated, they finally left on 7 July 1862, seven months after their intended rendezvous with Petherick.

Speke believed that if there was a river flowing north out of Lake Victoria it would almost certainly be the Nile, and that its discoverers would be assured of glory. Yet on the cusp of discovery, just days before he reached the river, he made an extraordinary decision. He ordered Grant to continue north to pave the expedition's way to the court of Kamrasi, king of Bunyoro, whilst he himself marched on to find the river. Only Grant, the obedient and dutiful friend, would have accepted such a command when their prize was so close. Later, when Speke was accused of gross egotism, the self-effacing, loyal Grant defended his friend. But at the time he was reluctant to follow Speke's orders. His diary entry hints at suppressed rage and, uncharacteristically, he had his favourite goatherd beaten for a trivial offence.

Two days after their parting, Speke was exulting in the discovery of a river he was sure was the Nile: 'Here at last I stood on the brink of the Nile; most beautiful was the scene, nothing could surpass it.' He followed the river south, upstream, to Lake Victoria and on 28 July he reached his goal: 'Though beautiful, the scene was not exactly what I expected; for the broad surface of the lake was shut out from view by a spur of hill, and the falls, about 12 feet deep, and 400 to 500 feet broad, were broken by rocks. Still it was a sight that attracted one for hours ...' He named the waterfall the Ripon Falls, after the president of the Royal Geographical Society, and concluded: 'The expedition had now performed its functions. I saw that old father Nile without any doubt rises in the Victoria N'yanza.' And that, as far as Speke was concerned, was that.

Elated, he hastened to join Grant, only to find him retreating out of Kamrasi's kingdom. The king was suspicious of the explorers and when he finally allowed them to enter his territory he held them there against their will. By now the two men simply wanted to get out and carry news of Speke's discovery home to Europe. While they were trapped by Kamrasi, Speke was told of another lake a

Opposite: Map of Speke and Grant's route along the western side of Lake Victoria.

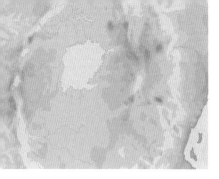

short march to the west, which was said to have large rivers flowing into and out of it. Its local name was the Luta Nzige, but in time it would be renamed Lake Albert. Weary and short of provisions, Speke chose not to investigate this lake, a mere ten-day march away. It was a serious mistake as it left the field open for competing theories about the source of the Nile. Perhaps Lake Tanganyika fed this new lake, which in turn fed the Nile? Maybe Burton was right after all?

Speke's original plan had been to follow the White Nile downstream, but cataracts and waterfalls made the river unnavigable and the expedition had to go north on foot. By now Speke and Grant had no heart left for pioneering and it was only by ignominiously tagging along with an ivory trader that they finished their journey. They entered Gondokoro on 15 February 1863, almost two years and five months after they had set out from Bagamoyo. They were 14 months late for their rendezvous with Petherick.

Petherick had long gone, but in his place they found a most unlikely couple: Samuel Baker and his young wife Florence. Speke and Baker were old friends and were glad to meet up again. 'What joy this was I can hardly tell. We could not talk fast enough, so overwhelmed were we both to meet again,' Speke wrote. There was a lot of news to exchange: Baker told of the death of Prince Albert, the prince consort, and the outbreak of Civil War in America; Speke gave the devastating news that he had largely solved the riddle of the Nile. Baker, who harboured ambitions to discover the source himself, was understandably disappointed.

On his way home, Speke cabled London: 'Inform Sir Roderick Murchison that all is well, that we are in Latitude 14°13' upon the Nile, and that the Nile is settled.' In fact, a great deal remained unresolved. Speke had achieved an enormous amount but he had not conclusively debunked all the counter-theories. As his critics later pointed out, although he had assumed he was making his way around the western edge of Lake Victoria, he had never proved it. He had followed the shore for only 80 km (50 miles) yet asserted that there was one vast lake, not two or even more. And he had not conscientiously followed the river downstream from Ripon Falls, but had crossed large stretches of land and, on regaining a river, had assumed it was the Nile. Indeed, he had returned to England with no irrefutable evidence that he had found the source of the Nile.

Right: Ripon Falls – a woodcut based on Speke's sketch. On seeing these falls Speke believed he had finally solved the puzzle of the Nile's source.

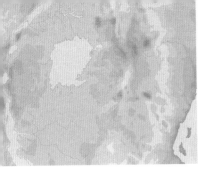

# LAKE ALBERT: A CONTROVERSIAL DISCOVERY

While Speke and Grant were making their way home, Samuel and Florence Baker were heading upstream. They believed there were still important discoveries to be made and their plan was to explore the area west of Lake Victoria and, in particular, the Luta Nzige – the lake Speke had heard about when he was in Bunyoro.

Samuel Baker had been born into an immense fortune and had never had to do anything as dull as earn a living. But he had a restless, adventuring spirit which, combined with unusual resourcefulness and practicality, made him good explorer material. He was also unconventional: after his first wife died he fell in love with and married Florence, a girl he had bought in a Turkish slave market. A Hungarian refugee, she adored Baker. He had saved her from an unthinkable fate and she rewarded him with devotion. The two were inseparable and, luckily for Baker, Florence was brave enough, tough enough and in love enough to follow him through the worst that nineteenth-century Africa had to throw at them.

In 1861 they had decided that they would like to participate in the exploration of the Nile's source. As Baker's family money gave them total independence they did not need the backing of scientific institutions, the Church or the government. They spent an initial year exploring tributaries of the Nile in Abyssinia (now Ethiopia) where Baker indulged in his favourite pastime – game shooting – and, having acquired basic Arabic, they travelled on up the Nile to Khartoum. In the mid-nineteenth century the city was a melting pot of races and cultures. It was also the hub of the northern slave and ivory routes, which brought with them all their associated barbarism and squalor. 'A more miserable, filthy and unhealthy place can hardly be imagined,' Baker wrote.

When he and Florence arrived in Khartoum he heard from the Royal Geographical Society that Petherick and his wife were presumed dead and that the two explorers, Speke and Grant, had been missing for over a year. Could he go and find them? The challenge appealed to Baker and, despite considerable opposition from the governor of Khartoum, he and Florence

Left: Samuel and Florence Baker in 1866. Self-funded, the Bakers followed the Nile upstream from Egypt to try to find its source. They suffered incredible hardships and were lucky to survive.

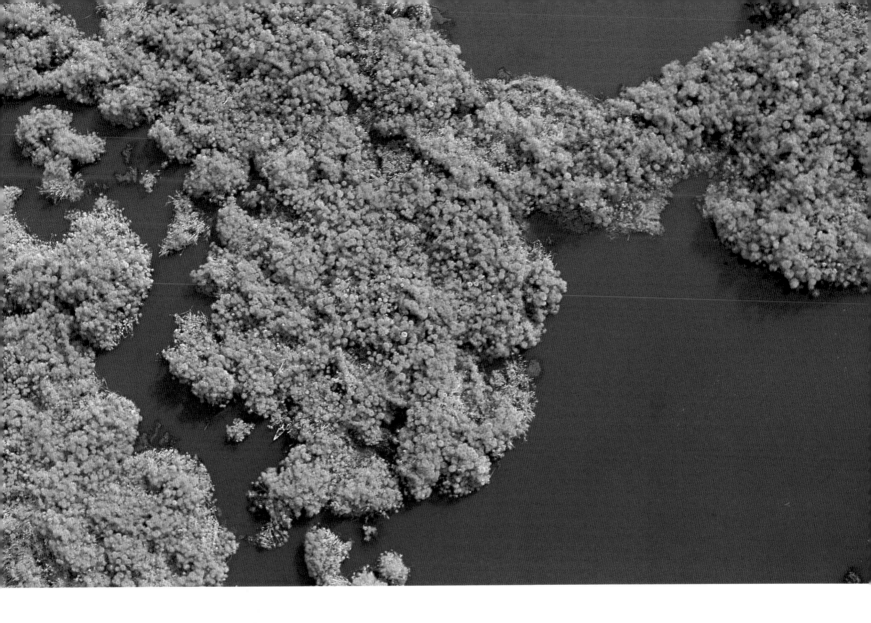

Above: Aerial view of a
papyrus swamp. The
Bakers fought their way
through hundreds of miles
of the Sudd without a
clear idea of what lay
ahead.

set sail for Gondokoro, to the south, on 18 December 1862. It was the start of what was to be
one of the most gruelling journeys of exploration yet undertaken.

After sailing through the desert for 800 km (500 miles) they entered the Sudd. This vast papyrus
swamp, with its rotting vegetation and patrolling crocodiles, the air humming with mosquitoes,
was as formidable a barrier to the Bakers as it had been to other explorers over the centuries.
However, with a fair wind and exceptional luck, they navigated its few clear channels and
passed through it in just 40 days. They arrived in Gondokoro in February 1863, just 12 days
before Speke and Grant, gaunt and weary, marched in from the south.

When Speke told them about the unexplored Luta Nzige the Bakers' enthusiasm for continuing
was rekindled. But their progress upstream to the kingdom of Bunyoro was agonizingly slow.
South of Gondokoro they were obliged to walk in order to circumvent the rapids that stretch for
more than 130 km (80 miles). Then, with their expedition weakened when many of their porters
deserted them, they were obliged to join forces with a Turkish slave and ivory trader, who

travelled fast when on the move but barely at all when acquiring his goods. Rape and pillage were everyday occurrences; Baker was appalled but could do little about it. In the end it took them ten gruelling months to cover the ground Speke and Grant had covered in three. During this time the Bakers suffered incredible hardships: their baggage animals died, their food ran out and they were reduced to eating grass, they both contracted malaria and were delirious in turn for weeks, and local people attacked them with poisoned arrows.

Kamrasi was now at war with his brother and, initially, would not let the Bakers into his kingdom. When he relented, Baker, half-dead from malaria, had to be carried into his court on a stretcher. Despite the physical condition of his guests, Kamrasi extracted an unusually large

THE SEARCH FOR THE SOURCE

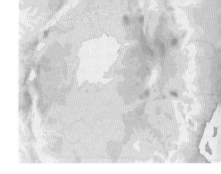

Left: The Nile crocodile's distribution is far wider than the Nile valley itself. This reptile is found right across sub-Saharan Africa and as far south as South Africa.

number of gifts. The king was not only greedy – he did not trust a man who would leave his own country and suffer unimaginable hardships simply to see a lake. After a short time he unexpectedly told Baker he could proceed to the lake with porters and provisions, but on one condition: he was to leave Florence behind. Baker would have a Bunyoro virgin in her place. Enraged, Baker lost all sense of diplomacy, pulled out his pistol, aimed it at Kamrasi's chest and threatened to shoot him. Florence, also incensed, rounded on the king with a torrent of insulting Arabic. Although Kamrasi did not understand a word of it, he let them both go.

They set out for the Luta Nzige, but once again their progress was hampered by the terrain. Florence nearly died of sunstroke, then Baker collapsed. Gradually they both gained strength

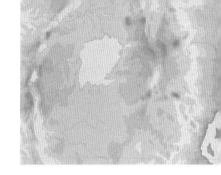

enough to continue. Finally, on 13 March, their guide told them they would see the lake on the morrow.

A year after leaving Gondokoro the Bakers finally reached their objective. Baker wrote:

*The day broke beautifully clear, and having crossed a deep valley between the hills, we toiled up the opposite slope. I hurried to the summit. The glory of our prize burst suddenly upon me! There, like a sea of quicksilver, lay far beneath the grand expanse of water – a boundless sea horizon on the south and south-west, glittering in the noonday sun, and on the west, at fifty or sixty miles' distance, blue mountains rose from the bosom of the lake to a height of about 7,000 feet above its level. It is impossible to describe the triumph of that moment … I felt too serious to vent my feelings in vain cheers for victory and I sincerely thanked God for having guided and supported us through all dangers to the good end.*

Baker named the lake 'Albert' after the late prince consort, and seemed convinced that its discovery was as important as that of Lake Victoria. But, weakened by his hardships and once again desperately short of provisions, he did not explore the full extent of the lake. As with Burton and Speke before him, this failure to map the inflows and outflows of his discovery would leave room for controversy back in London.

After turning for home the Bakers came across a large river that flowed into Lake Albert. This was assuredly Speke's Victoria Nile. But the elevation readings for Lake Victoria that Speke had given to Baker were considerably higher than those he himself had recorded on Lake Albert. Surely, somewhere between these two lakes there must be a huge waterfall? Unable to resist the temptation of so great a discovery, the Bakers pushed on up the river and less than 50 km (30 miles) upstream they found it – an explosion of water through a narrow cleft in the rock. Baker was delighted:

*The fall of water was snow-white, which had a superb effect as it contrasted with the dark cliffs that walled the river, while the graceful palms of the tropics and wild plantains perfected the beauty of the view. This was the greatest waterfall of the Nile, and in honour of the distinguished President of the Royal Geographical Society, I named it the Murchison Falls, as the most important object throughout the entire course of the river.*

Although elated with their find, the Bakers were soon faced with the difficulties of getting home. It was another miserable journey. It took them two months to struggle back to Kamrasi's court –

Opposite: Uganda kob live on floodplain grasslands, preferring to feed on short, palatable grass near water. They provided easy meat for the early gun-bearing travellers.

where they were greeted by a different king. It turned out that the real Kamrasi, suspicious of their intentions, had planted a brother in his place when they first arrived. The real king now proceeded to strip the malaria-stricken travellers of their remaining goods. With war raging around them, the Bakers remained virtual prisoners for six frustrating months.

They left Kamrasi's court with an Arab slaving party and reached Gondokoro after an absence of two years. They had long since been given up for dead. Crossing the Sudd, they were held up by unfavourable winds and a plague killed some of their remaining men. In Khartoum sad news awaited them: Speke had died in England in 1864, in a shooting accident.

The Bakers reached London in 1865, five years after having set out, and though they were celebrated on their return – they were awarded the Royal Geographical Society Gold Medal and Baker was knighted – they had done little to clear up the controversy surrounding the source of the Nile. Their discovery of Lake Albert meant there was another lake to add to the puzzle, a lake whose inflows, outflows and extent had not been ascertained. If it was as large as Baker claimed, Lake Albert and not Lake Victoria could easily be regarded as the source of the Nile. Moreover, like Speke and Grant, the Bakers had not followed the river that flowed north out of the lake, so it was possible that it was not, after all, the Nile.

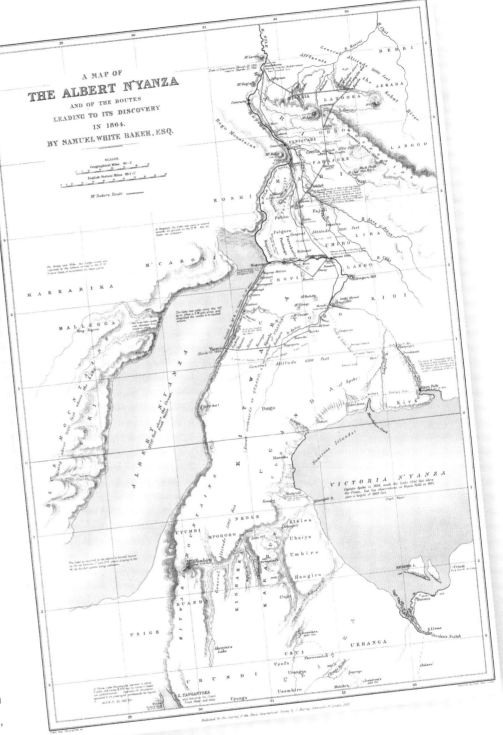

Opposite: Murchison Falls. The White Nile contracts from a width of 50 m (164 feet) to just 7 m (23 feet) as it cascades over the falls, creating an immensely powerful water surge.

Above: Baker's map exaggerated the size and therefore the significance of his primary discovery, Lake Albert, which he reached in 1864.

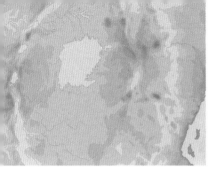

# A LEGENDARY MEETING

Even before the Bakers returned to London the debate as to exactly where the source of the Nile was to be found had been rekindled, and on Speke's death the Royal Geographical Society had resolved to act. In May 1865, while the Bakers were still in Khartoum, Sir Roderick Murchison announced that the society was sending Dr David Livingstone to settle, once and for all, the question of the source of the Nile.

Livingstone was first and foremost a medical missionary – but one with an interest in discovery. He was kind and gentle, but determined, and many of his contemporaries felt he had qualities of true greatness. He had discovered the Victoria Falls on the Zambezi river in 1855, and after the publication of his *Missionary Travels* in 1857 he had become the most celebrated and popular of African explorers. He had recently returned from a traumatic six-year expedition up the Zambezi, during which his wife had died.

His brief was an extensive one. He was to explore the area around Lake Tanganyika and, in particular, was to determine whether the Ruzizi river flowed into or out of it. If it flowed out of the lake and northwards (as Burton now believed), he was to see if it flowed into Lake Albert. If this was the case, and if the river flowing out of Lake Albert was the Nile, Burton and later Baker, not Speke and Grant, would have discovered the Nile's source.

**Above:** Dr David Livingstone in 1864. Although he spent most of his working life in Africa, he was a much-admired household name in Victorian Britain.

Livingstone's expedition did not achieve its objectives, but it played an important part in ending the slave trade in this part of Africa. After leaving Zanzibar in 1866, Livingstone took a year to reach the southern shores of Lake Tanganyika. Two years later, after some exploration and missionary work to the west, on the Lualaba river and in the swamps of Bangweulu, he retreated to Ujiji, skeletally thin, ill and exhausted. Here he was devastated to find that the expected store of fresh supplies from the coast had been plundered, and that the two most important items – quinine and mail – had gone. Returning to the Lualaba river (the exploration of which, he obstinately believed, would reveal the secret of the source of the Nile), Livingstone witnessed a horrifying massacre. Before his eyes, trigger-happy Arab slavers murdered some 400 Africans. When his detailed account of this atrocity eventually reached the wider world, it galvanized public opinion against slavery and the sultan of Zanzibar was forced to close the slave market on the island for ever.

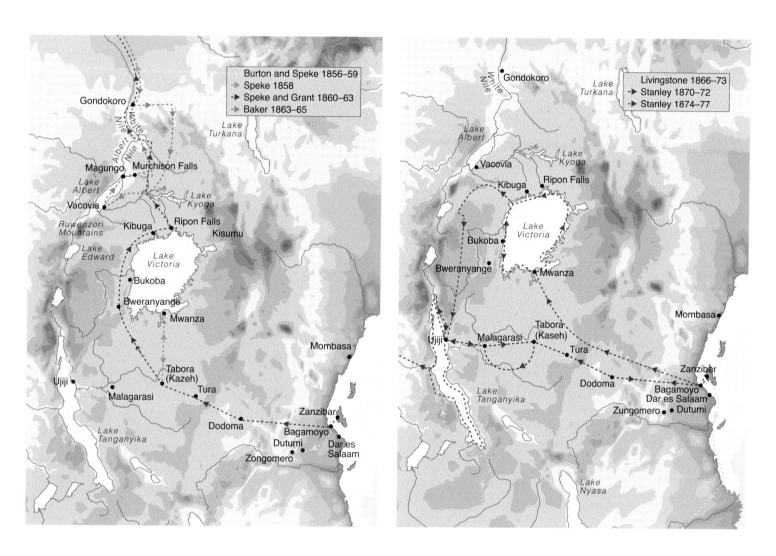

Above left: Map showing the routes of Burton's, Speke's and Baker's expeditions.

Above right: Map showing the routes of Livingstone's and Stanley's expeditions.

Disheartened, bereft of supplies and very ill, Livingstone struggled back to Ujiji once more. It was here, on 10 November 1871, that an event took place that is possibly the best known in all African exploration: Henry Morton Stanley found Livingstone.

Stanley's description of the famous meeting is delightfully honest:

*Selim said to me, 'I see the Doctor, sir. Oh, what an old man! He has got a white beard!'*
*And I – what would I not have given for a bit of friendly wilderness, where, unseen, I might vent*
*my joy in some mad freak, such as idiotically biting my hand, turning a somersault, or slashing*
*at trees, in order to allay those exciting feelings that were well-nigh uncontrollable. My heart*
*beats fast, but I must not let my face betray my emotions, lest it shall detract from the dignity*
*of a white man appearing under such extraordinary circumstances.*

Above: Stanley finds Livingstone – one of the best-known moments of African exploration.

So I did that which I thought was most dignified. I pushed back the crowds, and, passing from the rear, walked down a living avenue of people, until I came in front of the semicircle of Arabs, before which stood 'the white man with the grey beard'. As I advanced slowly towards him I noticed he was pale, looked wearied, had grey whiskers and moustache, wore a bluish cap with a faded gold band around it, had on a red-sleeved waistcoat, and a pair of grey tweed trousers. I would have run to him, only I was a coward in the presence of such a mob – would have embraced him, but that I did not know how he would receive me. So I did what moral

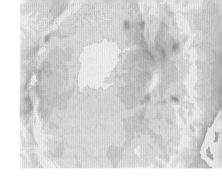

*cowardice and false pride suggested was the best thing – walked deliberately up to him, took off my hat, and said, 'Dr Livingstone, I presume?' 'Yes,' he said, with a kind smile, lifting his cap slightly.*

*I replaced my hat on my head, and he replaced his cap, and we both grasped hands, and then I said aloud: 'I thank God, Doctor, I have been permitted to see you.'*

*He answered, 'I feel thankful that I am here to welcome you.'*

Stanley was a newspaper journalist, fast making a name for himself at the *New York Herald*. Long before he arrived in Ujiji, he had been summoned to a hotel in Paris by the newspaper's proprietor, James Gordon Bennett, and given a string of assignments. He was to report on the opening of the Suez Canal, visit Jerusalem, Constantinople, the battlefields of the Crimea and the Caspian Sea, and to travel through Persia to India, all the while sending back accounts that would interest the American public. 'After that,' he was instructed, 'you can start looking round for Livingstone. If he is dead, bring back every possible proof of his death.' Remarkably, Stanley fulfilled this brief in all its detail. But the final instruction – to find Livingstone – would change his life for ever.

Born out of wedlock, Stanley was raised in Dickensian poverty in a Welsh workhouse. He escaped a life of drudgery by working as a cabin boy on a ship bound for New Orleans. Here he was taken in by an American merchant, from whom he took his name and his nationality. His globetrotting assignments for the *New York Herald* capped a remarkably adventurous life in America. Stanley had fought on both sides in the Civil War, served in the US Navy and had covered the country's expansion west as a journalist.

His arrival in Ujiji revived Livingstone's hopes of finishing his explorations. Stanley, for his part, was leading a huge expedition with surplus supplies and was more than willing to help resolve whether the Ruzizi river flowed into or out of Lake Tanganyika. So he and Livingstone set out on 16 November 1871 and made their way north up the lake. Only 12 days later, at the end of the lake, they found, to Livingstone's great disappointment, that the river flowed *into* Lake Tanganyika. However, he would not give up, and conjectured that the river flowing out of Lake Tanganyika to the west would lead to the Lualaba and thence to the Nile.

**Left:** Henry Morton Stanley in 1874. A journalist backed by an American newspaper, Stanley brought considerable resources and a ruthless efficiency to the search for the source of the Nile.

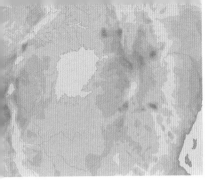

The two men returned to Ujiji, then walked east to Tabora, some 480 km (300 miles) away, where Stanley had stored yet more supplies. He took what he needed for his return trip to the coast and gave the remainder to Livingstone so that the missionary could continue his explorations. Stanley and Livingstone parted in Tabora on 14 March 1872. Although their names are bound together in the history of African exploration, they never met again.

In May 1872 Stanley reached Zanzibar. The news of his meeting with Livingstone caused a sensation around the world, and on his arrival in England the naturalized American was fêted by his native country, receiving numerous honours and medals. Meanwhile, Livingstone's health was deteriorating. He waited five months for new porters whom Stanley sent up from the coast, then headed south to Lake Tanganyika, still believing it was the true source of the Nile. On 1 May 1873, a little over a year after Stanley had headed home, Livingstone was found dead, kneeling as if in prayer by his bed.

What follows is perhaps the most remarkable tale in all African exploration. The two faithful servants who found Livingstone, Susi and Chuma, decided that his body should return to Britain. They cut out his heart and other organs and buried them under a tree. They dried his body in the sun for two weeks, wrapped it in cloth and bark and strung it on a pole. With 60 men who had remained with Livingstone to the end, they set out for the coast, some 2400 km (1500 miles) away. At Tabora they met an expedition that had set out to look for Livingstone and the news of their strange journey was sent on to Zanzibar. When they reached Bagamoyo, after 11 months, HMS *Vulture* was waiting to take Livingstone's body to England. There it was carried through streets lined with mourning Londoners to its final resting place in Westminster Abbey.

Stanley was also in mourning. Although he and Livingstone were very different characters – where Stanley was egocentric and brutal, Livingstone was gentle, generous and kindly – in the weeks they were in each other's company they had become firm friends.

## AN EPIC EXPEDITION

Stanley had lost the one friend he revered above all others. But it was this loss that had a dramatic impact on his ambitions: it galvanized him into returning to Africa a second time. He resolved to take up Livingstone's baton and put to rest all remaining doubts about the source of the Nile.

He set about researching the expedition with his characteristic thoroughness. He read every available account of central Africa, including those of Burton, Speke, Grant and Baker, and looked at every map that had ever been published on the area. He then set out three objectives. First, he would circumnavigate Lake Victoria to see if it was really one large lake and to confirm whether or not the Ripon Falls was the only outlet. Second, he would circumnavigate Lake Tanganyika to test Burton's theory that there was a river running out of the lake that became the Nile. Third, he would find and follow the Lualaba river to its mouth, wherever that might be, to fulfil Livingstone's quest.

**Above:** By the time the European explorers started their search for the Nile's source in earnest, much of the Nile basin had already been opened up by Turkish and Arab ivory traders.

Backed jointly by the *New York Herald* and the *Daily Telegraph*, Stanley had vast resources at his disposal. He left England for Zanzibar in August 1874, just months after Livingstone had been buried. By November of the same year he was on his way from Zanzibar to Bagamoyo. It was the largest expedition central Africa had ever seen. Stanley had a full 7 tonnes of provisions and 356 men to transport them. He also had with him the 12-m (39-foot) boat *Lady Alice*, which was carried in sections. This small army wound its way inland and three and half months later was on the shores of Lake Victoria.

Stanley lost 100 men through desertion, sickness and clashes with hostile tribes, and one of his three British companions perished. (The other two would also lose their lives before the end of the journey.) This first leg of the expedition set up a pattern that characterized all Stanley's travels. He covered ground fast, using brutal discipline to deal with mutinous porters. He met

Below: Mountain gorillas would have been far more widespread in Stanley's time than they are today. But they are such secretive animals that Stanley may never have realized they were there.

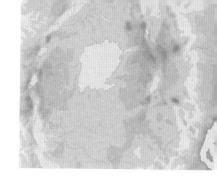

force with force and killed local people who resisted his progress through their country, leaving a path of destruction behind him. And he was prepared to suffer huge losses amongst his own men. Such methods could not have been more directly opposed to those of Livingstone, the man he so admired.

On reaching Lake Victoria, Stanley set off in the *Lady Alice* with 11 men, leaving his remaining two companions behind. Three weeks later, having mapped the east coast of the lake, he arrived at the Ripon Falls. On 5 April 1875 he was taken to meet Mtesa – and met a man apparently quite unlike the vicious despot Speke had described. In fact, the Bugandan king had not changed greatly: shortly before Stanley arrived an emissary from the Sudan was honoured with the sacrifice of 30 men. Mtesa had, however, grown to understand the rudiments of politics and diplomacy.

Unlike his predecessors, Stanley was not held by Mtesa and by 6 May 1875 he was back on the southern shores of Lake Victoria, reunited with the party he had left behind. In 57 days he had circumnavigated the lake, sailed and rowed some 1600 km (1000 miles), and proved that Victoria was, indeed, one lake. He also confirmed that the Ripon Falls was its only outlet and that the Kagera river was its major feeder stream. Stanley was generous in his appraisal of Speke:

*Speke has now the full glory of having discovered the largest inland sea on the continent of Africa, also its principal affluent as well as its outlet. I must also give him credit for having understood the geography of the countries we travelled through better than any of those who so persistently opposed his hypothesis …*

In July what remained of the expedition after desertions and death made its way back north to Buganda. Here Stanley helped Mtesa fight a battle with the Wavuma before reminding the king that he had promised him an escort through Bunyoro, en route to Lake Albert and a rumoured smaller lake (now called Lake Edward) to the south. Mtesa provided 4000 soldiers, but inevitably they were regarded as a hostile force by local tribes, and Stanley was forced to abandon his plan to explore Lake Albert. Nevertheless, before turning back, he managed to reach the east rim of the western Rift Valley where he saw a small lake (now called Lake George), only 16 km (10 miles) in diameter.

Stanley headed south to Karagwe and spent a month in Rumanika's court before setting off for Lake Tanganyika. In June 1876 he launched the *Lady Alice* at Ujiji, and spent two months circumnavigating the lake. He found no major outlet that could be the start of the Nile, so Burton's theory was finally proved wrong.

It was two years since Stanley had set out from the coast, and he had accomplished two of his goals. Now, with a diminished team, he set out to achieve his final goal: to follow the Lualaba river to the west, in Livingstone's footsteps and beyond. Stanley embarked on a journey that became legendary from his description of it in his book *Through the Dark Continent* (1878). The Lualaba fed not into the Nile but into the Congo river – and when he had traced its course to the sea, he had crossed the continent of Africa from east to west. He and his men suffered relentlessly. They were shipwrecked, half-starved, attacked by tribes along the banks of the Congo and lost their supplies. Stanley's last remaining British companion died, as did his faithful bearer, who was like a son to him. The bedraggled expedition eventually arrived at the mouth of the river on the west African coast 999 days after leaving Zanzibar. Of the 356 men who had started out, only 114 remained. Stanley sailed with them around the Cape of Good Hope to Zanzibar before returning to England in 1877.

**Above:** Stanley twice crossed Africa through the forests of the Congo basin: '…penetrating a trackless wild for the first time the march was at a funereal pace, in some places at the rate of 400 yards an hour…'

**Opposite:** Stanley admired the 'marvelous agility' of monkeys, such as the black and white colobus, who hurled 'their tiny bodies through the air across yawning chasms …'

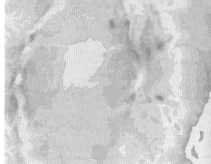

By now the White Nile itself had been charted. In 1874, an American soldier and explorer, Charles Chaillé-Long, chief of staff to General Gordon, who was then in the service of the khedive of Egypt, had followed its flow from the Ripon Falls through a previously undiscovered lake, Lake Kyoga, to the Karuma Falls, where Speke and the Bakers had been before him. And in 1876 another of Gordon's men, Romolo Gessi, had circumnavigated Lake Albert, proving the Bakers' claims about its size to be vastly exaggerated.

Stanley's association with the Nile was not at an end. More than ten years later, in 1889, he was on a mission to rescue Mehmed Emin Pasha, governor of Equatoria – at that time a province of the Egyptian Sudan. Emin Pasha had been cut off near Lake Albert by the Mahdist revolt of

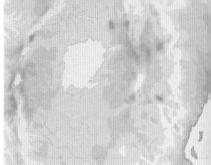

1882. Stanley reached the lake from the west, through the Congo, and became the first European to see Lake Edward, which he named after the Prince of Wales. He also saw the snowy peaks of the fabled Mountains of the Moon. Stanley realized that the entire catchment of this snow-covered range drained into Lake Albert through the Semliki river, whether via Lake George or Lake Edward. This, then, was surely a sister source of the Nile to Speke's Lake Victoria and Kagera river? Stanley wrote:

*Another emotion is that inspired by the thought that in one of the darkest corners of the earth, shrouded by perpetual mist, brooding under the eternal storm-clouds, surrounded by darkness and mystery, there has been hidden to this day a giant among the mountains,*

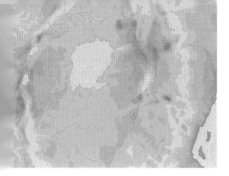

*the melting snow of whose tops has been for some fifty centuries most vital to the peoples of Egypt.*

Stanley's 50 centuries was an understatement. The peoples of Egypt had been relying on meltwater from the Ruwenzoris for over 7000 years.

The Ruwenzoris, or 'rainmakers', provide a crucial link in the feeding of the Nile via Lake Albert. They are the wettest mountains in Africa, with an average annual rainfall of about 2000 mm (78 inches). The prevailing moisture-laden winds blowing across Africa drop their load either as snow or rain on the Ruwenzoris and, importantly, the water is held there. Snow settling on the tops of the peaks compacts into their glaciers and is held as ice, melting only slowly. Rain is held in lakes in the glacier-carved deep valleys or in bogs in the shallower valleys. And the dense forest on the mountainsides, draped in moss and lichen, catches fog and holds its own share of the water. This sodden reservoir drip-feeds the streams and rivers that run out of the mountains and thus ameliorates the impact of the dry and rainy seasons that occur in other parts of the White Nile catchment.

Stanley did not have time to venture into the Ruwenzoris in 1889 when he first saw them, but he recognized their importance as he marched out to the coast of east Africa. He returned from this last expedition to triumphant acclaim. Queen Victoria, Leopold of Belgium, the kaiser of Germany, the khedive of Egypt and the president of the United States all commended him in telegrams. The world went mad for Stanley. But he went into hiding to write *In Darkest Africa* before emerging to receive his accolades.

Stanley had his critics. Amongst other failings they cited his loss of nearly 350 bearers in the Congo and the brutal way in which he dealt with wayward men, often lashing them to death. But their voices were drowned by roars of applause. In 1890, with the publication of his book, Stanley was the most admired and greatest of all living explorers. At last he had proved himself and was accepted by society at large. Honorary degrees were forthcoming and he became a British subject again in 1892, and a Member of Parliament in 1895. In 1899, he was knighted.

Determining the source of the Nile had proved to be a great deal more complicated than had, at first, been imagined. The Victorian explorers set out on their expeditions expecting to find Ptolemy's snow-capped mountains and two lakes (which the German missionaries Johann Rebmann and Jacob Erhardt had joined into one large slug-like lake). Burton was wrong about Lake Tanganyika being the source, while Speke discovered Lake Victoria and guessed,

correctly, that this was the river's reservoir. The Bakers muddied the waters by claiming that Lake Albert was as big as Lake Victoria and should therefore have equal status, if not a greater claim to be the river's source because it extended further south. Livingstone added little to the picture except that, with Stanley, he confirmed that the river at the north end of Lake Tanganyika did not feed Lake Albert. Stanley recognized Speke's contribution in finding Lake Victoria and the Ripon Falls, and for a long time the lake was regarded as the source, but he also recognized the part the Ruwenzoris played in the system. Rather than finding one large lake from which the Nile issued, the courageous explorers had discovered a complicated system of mountains, lakes, rivers and swamps – all of which ultimately end up feeding the Nile.

The White Nile has two main drainage systems: one to the northwest, which embraces the western Rift Valley and the Ruwenzoris; the other further south and east, which includes Lake Victoria. This larger system drains a huge area encompassing much of Burundi, Rwanda, northern Tanzania, western Kenya and Uganda. At its centre is the great reservoir of Lake Victoria, into which all the rivers drain and out of which only one river – the Victoria Nile – flows. Burundi lays claim to the spring waters of the Kagera, Lake Victoria's largest feeder river, but today people recognize the scale and importance of both drainage basins.

Previous page: Margherita Peak on Mount Stanley – at 5109 m (16,761 feet) the highest peak of the Ruwenzori range. These glaciers form the highest of the Nile's sources.

Above: Water falling as rain or snow is trapped in the Ruwenzori glaciers as ice. These equatorial glaciers are today gradually receding.

Right: The Ruwenzori Mountains are among the wettest places on the continent, with rain falling almost daily.

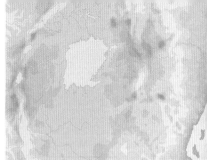

The smaller system to the northwest drains much of the Virungas (a chain of volcanic mountains south of Lake Edward), the Ruwenzoris to the north and the land in between. This is all part of the western Rift Valley along which the Semliki river carries water from Lakes George and Edward to Lake Albert. In Lake Albert, waters from the Semliki and the Victoria Nile meet and flow north as the White Nile.

The Nile is a remarkably young river and its formation was due to a series of lucky geological events. For many millions of years both Ethiopia and the Sudan drained into the Red Sea and the Indian Ocean; the way north was blocked by the Nubian massif. At the same time, water from the equatorial plateau, a region covering much of Uganda and Tanzania, drained west into the Congo basin or east into the Indian Ocean; only a little drained north into the Sudd.

Above: The Bujuku is just one of a number of rivers flowing out of the Ruwenzori range; its waters meet those from Lake Victoria and ultimately form the Nile.

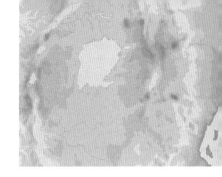

The creation of the Great Rift Valley, which occurred between 12 and 2 million years ago, saw great changes to the topography of eastern Africa. The equatorial plateau was cut by two rift valleys, one to the west and one to the east. Waters cascading off the Ethiopian and equatorial plateaus began to be redirected towards what we know as the Nile, but it took a long time for them to find their way north to Egypt.

In the western rift, landlocked basins began to fill with water; Lake Tanganyika formed, as did Lakes Albert, Edward and George. The edges of the equatorial plateau were forced up, creating an internally drained shallow depression, which also began to fill with water. Rivers such as the Kagera, which had hitherto flowed west to the Congo, reversed their flow and headed east. Lake Victoria was born. As the topography of the region changed so did the climate, resulting in more and more water finding its way into this spreading lake.

High in Ethiopia, where massive lava flows blocked and dammed rivers, new courses were eroded. The Blue Nile gorge was formed in this way and over hundreds of thousands of years, powered by the full force of the rains draining from the Ethiopian Highlands, the river cut its way through the mountains and down into the deserts of the Sudan, through the Nubian massif and into Egypt.

During the wettest periods of interglacial activity Lake Victoria may have temporarily drained north via the Sudd into Egypt. But it was not until the end of the last ice age, some 12,500 years ago, that the region received and retained so much rain that Lake Victoria spilled north via the Ripon Falls to Lake Albert, and Lake Albert spilled north to the Sudd. The Sudd had dried up during the glacial period, so there was little vegetation to hold the water and it found a route north to Egypt.

The Nile, as we know it today, was formed by rains from both the equatorial plateau and the Ethiopian Highlands. It received a steady, year-round flow from central Africa, where Lake Victoria, the Ruwenzoris and the Sudd acted as huge reservoirs, and an annual flood from Ethiopia, which had no such reservoirs but simply delivered the rains as they fell, along with a cargo of precious, rich volcanic soil. Some 7000 years ago, the stage was set for nomads moving in from the drying Sahara desert to settle along its banks – the birth of the ancient Egyptian civilization.

Opposite: Muhavura volcano forms part of the Virunga range, a group of volcanic mountains that borders the southwest corner of the Nile basin.

Overleaf: At Juba in southern Sudan the mountains and rolling hills of the upper reaches of the river disappear and the landscape becomes flat. Here the river spreads out into the Sudd before finding its way through the desert to the Mediterranean Sea.

# ACKNOWLEDGEMENTS

This book and the television series it accompanies are, of course, inextricably linked. In researching the series we gleaned much of the knowledge needed to write the book, and in writing the book we discovered new aspects to stories that became important in the latter stages of filming. Our thanks, therefore, must go to all those who contributed to the wider *Nile* project, not just those directly responsible for the production of these pages.

Our thanks go first to our cameraman, Richard Kirby, who recognized the great potential of the Nile as a subject. Few people, if any, can have travelled the Nile from its diverse sources to its mouth in the Mediterranean Sea, but Richard, who spent the best part of a year in Africa, has come near to doing just that. We owe him a huge debt of gratitude for interpreting our emerging ideas and bringing them back home on film. He was accompanied by George Chan and Pip Lawson who dug out the many stories we filmed and confidently and successfully led expeditions into the remoter parts of the Nile basin.

We also owe a sincere thank you to the production team who stayed in the office, master-minding the day-to-day operations and planning shoots. Sue Loder, Amy Freeman and Jo Lethbridge packed us off, manned the money box while we were away, and gave us a warm welcome back. Their unerring good humour and attention to detail kept us all going. In the latter stages of production, Mike Gunton expertly steered us through the pitfalls of storytelling. Editors Martin Elsbury, Jo Payne and Nigel Buck deftly crafted the films, and Kate Hopkins, Lucy Rutherford, Graham Wild and Andrew Wilson created the world of sound that brings them alive. David Mitcham kindly wrote the music that so enhances the films.

In researching the project we were able to call on a great number of eminent historians and scientists. In particular we would like to thank the following: John Romer, Dr Fekri Hassan, Mindy Baha El-Din, Dr Moustafa Fouda for their help on Egypt, ancient and modern; Paul Wilson, Professor Wendy James and Dr Douglas Johnson for sharing their knowledge of Sudan; and Dr Zelealem Tefera and Dr Chadden Hunter who assisted with Ethiopia. For expertise on Uganda we would like to thank Achilles Byaruhanga, Julius Arinaitwe, Lauren and Colin Chapman, Andy Plumptre, David Pluth, Henry Osmaston and Wilhelm Moeller. Back home the Royal Geographical Society gave us open access to their knowledge and their map room.

During the year of production numerous people contributed to make each trip a success. Romany and Mary Helmy, Ramy Helmy, George Pagaloutos, Richard and Julia Kemp,

Mulualem Gelaye, Jane and Paul Goldring, Herbert Matte and Josia Makwalo all deserve our sincerest thanks.

We would also like to thank Deirdre O'Day for finding many of the photographs that illustrate this book, Bobby Birchall for designing the pages, Linda Blakemore for art direction and Martin Redfern, the editor, whose patience with us knew no bounds.

# PICTURE CREDITS

BBC Worldwide would like to thank the following for providing photographs and for permission to reproduce copyright material. While every effort has been made to trace and acknowledge copyright holders, we would like to apologize should there have been any errors or omissions.

The Annan Gallery, Glasgow: 138; Ardea London: © Andy Teare 44, © P. Morris 82; The Art Archive: 63, © Dagli Orti 39; The British Museum: 23; © George Chan: 1, 3, 4, 5g, 6–7, 29, 45, 50, 52, 94, 102, 104, 105 (above), 106–7; Corbis: 26–7, © Jacques Langevin 72, © Nevada Wier 108–9; The Fotomas Index: 111 (inset), 121–3, 128–9, 130, 140; © Chadden Hunter: 92; Images of Africa Photobank: © David Keith Jones 134, © Ursula Reif 148–9, © Wilhelm Möller 150–1; © Andrea Jemolo: 5b (inset), 21 (inset), 37 (left); © Richard and Julia Kemp: 5c (inset), 65 (inset), 78, 80–1, 84–5, 86 (below), 88–9; © Richard Kirby: 12–13, 14, 86 (above), 100–1, 124–5, 131; © Philippa Lawson: 5e, 110–11, 154–7; © Jürgen Liepe: 28 (below), 56–7; © Mark Linfield: 98; Mary Evans Picture Library: 141; © Gavin Maxwell: 5a, 20–1, 24, 25, 31, 33, 35, 37 (right), 46, 60–1; The National Portrait Gallery: 114; Naturepl.com: © Staffan Widstrand 30, 146, © Ron O'Connor 42–3, © Peter Blackwell 53, © Ingo Arndt 54, 99, © Bruce Davidson 83, 113, 136, 158, © Anup Shah 105 (below), © Tony Heald 132–3; Oxford Scientific Films Ltd: 95, © Liz Bomford 36, © Mark Deebles & Victoria Stone 77, © Joe McDonald/AA 87, © Konrad Wothe 147, © Richard Packwood 152–3; © Royal Geographical Society: 5f (inset), 115, 116, 117, 126, 137; Science Photo Library Ltd: © John Reader 2, 74–5, © Earth Satellite Corporation 34, © Karl H. Switak 43, © Peter Chadwick 118, © Joe McDonald/Okapia 144; © Tim Scoones: 5d, 8–9, 15, 16–19, 64–5, 67–70, 73, 90–1, 96–7; © Jeremy Stafford–Deitsch: 47, 48–9, 51; Still Pictures: © Toby Adamson 71; The Travel Library: 143; Werner Forman Archive: 59, © Dr. E. Strouhal 40; Woodfall Wild Images: © David Woodfall 160–1.

# INDEX